WANDA E. BRUNSTETTER'S

Amish Friends LIFE HACKS

Hundreds of Tips for Cooking, Cleaning, Gardening, Wellness, and More

BARBOUR
PUBLISHING

© 2023 by Wanda E. Brunstetter

Print ISBN 978-1-63609-693-3

All scripture quotations are taken from the King James Version of the Bible.

Cover top image: © 2020 Doyle Yoder, www.dypinc.com

Published by Barbour Publishing, Inc., 1810 Barbour Drive, Uhrichsville, OH 44683, www.barbourbooks.com

Our mission is to inspire the world with the life-changing message of the Bible.

ecpa Member of the
Evangelical Christian
Publishers Association

Printed in China.

CONTENTS

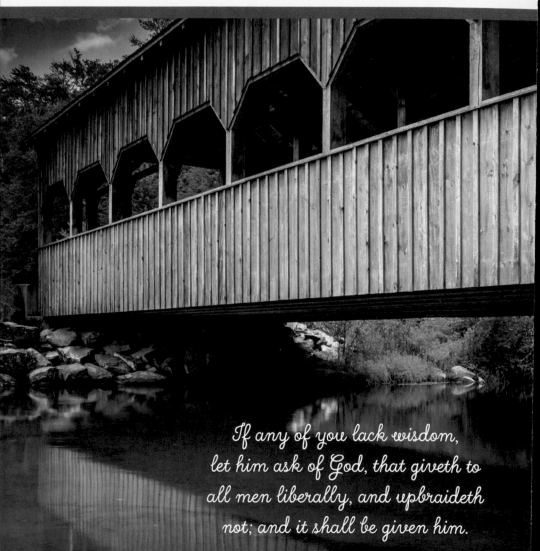

*If any of you lack wisdom,
let him ask of God, that giveth to
all men liberally, and upbraideth
not; and it shall be given him.*

JAMES 1:5

INTRODUCTION

Amish History

The Amish and Mennonites are direct descendants of the Anabaptists, a group that emerged from the Reformation in Switzerland in 1525 and developed separately in Holland a few years later. Anabaptists believed adults must be baptized (even if baptized as infants) after a confession of faith and only the baptized should partake in Communion, which the established Catholic and Protestant churches took offense to. They also maintained that the baptized should remain separate from anything perceived to be evil of the world, should have pastors from among them who were of good repute but also capable of being disciplined by the church, should not partake in violence such as war, and should not swear an oath. They also came to believe that the government and the church should have no interaction, which opened them up to harassment by government agencies.

Most Anabaptists eventually became identified as Mennonites, after prominent Dutch leader Menno Simons. The word *Amish* comes from Jacob Ammann, an influential leader who in 1693 led a group that separated from the Mennonite churches to follow even stricter teachings and practices of excommunication. Driven by persecution from their homes in Switzerland and Germany, hundreds of Mennonites began to immigrate to North America, first settling in Germantown, Pennsylvania, in 1683, becoming among the first to formally protest against the practice of slavery. The Amish were later welcomed in Pennsylvania by William Penn and first settled there around 1760.

Amish Today

As Amish settlements continued to grow and seek more land, new Amish communities were started in many parts of the United States and Canada, and new ones continue to appear. The Amish population has grown to over 370,000 in the United States. Pennsylvania is home to the majority of Amish with concentration in and around Lancaster County, while Ohio (primarily in and around Holmes County) is a close second in total number of Amish. Other notable settlements of Amish are located in Indiana, Wisconsin, New York, Michigan, Missouri, Kentucky, Iowa, and Illinois, though they can be found in many other states also.

While all Amish believe in the authority of the scriptures and adhere to the regulation of their *Ordnung* (church rules), their willingness to stand apart from the rest of the world shows through their simple, plain way of living. And though their outward appearance of dress, transportation, and rules of order would make them appear frozen in time, they do continually adapt to changes in society, including adopting some new technologies. For example, many Amish will now use electricity and phones in their businesses but still not in their homes. Each community will adapt at different rates as the leadership determines, and many communities differ in practices or rules, style of clothing, design of their homes and outbuildings, and types of buggies.

Amish Wisdom

Over the twenty-plus years I've been writing in the Amish genre, my husband and I have become close friends with many Amish people, and they are like family to us. We visit them often, and they have come to our home to spend time with us. We also keep in touch through letters, phone calls, and fun gatherings in Sarasota, Florida.

Spending quality time with our Amish friends has given me insights into their lives, and I've learned a lot of interesting information and tips they incorporate into their daily lives. One time, when we had been invited to an Amish friend's wedding, we stopped by the bride's home a few days before the big event. I was impressed with the speed and efficiency with which everyone worked together to prepare for the meal that would follow the wedding service. I learned something new as I watched some of the women preparing pineapples that would be included in the fruit salad to be served at the meal. They laid the pineapples on their sides, and without using knives, they grabbed the crown top and twisted to remove it. Then the pineapples were placed upside down in boxes to ripen further and become sweeter until time to cut them for the salad.

Our Amish friends enjoy passing along to the next generation the tips, recipes, and shortcuts they have learned from their parents and grandparents. Most of their baking is done from scratch and often without following a recipe closely. One day, after eating a delicious angel cream pie at one of our Amish friends' homes, I asked if she would share the recipe with me. When she wrote the directions on a sheet of paper, I was surprised to see that she hadn't included the time needed for baking the pie. Instead, she'd written, "Bake until a little shaky." My friend understood what that meant, because she'd made the pie many times and had learned the definition of "a little shaky" from her mother.

One thing that has left a huge impression on me is the wisdom my Amish friends impart to their children, grandchildren, and even to me as their friend. At first I wondered where so much wisdom came from, but it didn't take long to realize it comes from praying and spending time in God's Word, which they practice faithfully in their daily lives and walking with the Lord.

Amish children get training at home and in school. Girls learn to cook, sew, and manage a household. Boys learn how to care for the family's livestock and usually apprentice in a trade. I have visited many Amish schoolhouses over the years and seen for myself how well the children are taught. By the time an Amish child graduates from school, after completing the eighth grade, they have an education that is equal to, if not higher, than an English child who graduates from twelve grades. What the Amish learn in childhood is carried into their adult lives. In addition to their school education, they learn to be forgiving, helpful, hardworking, responsible, faithful, prayerful, problem solvers, prudent with their money, humble, kind, truthful, and obedient to God's commands.

The thing I appreciate most about my Amish friends is the wisdom they have concerning spiritual matters and how to conduct themselves as Christians. Although they certainly do not consider themselves perfect, the Amish people we know personally have a strong faith in God that is reflected in the way they live. Many times, while going through difficult situations, I have reached out to Amish friends for prayer and advice. Several of our friends are ministers in their church districts and have a responsibility to study the scriptures and minister to those in their congregation. What a blessing it is to have Amish friends who freely impart their love and wisdom.

I hope you will find some of their wisdom shared within these pages to be enjoyable and beneficial.

Blessings,
Wanda E. Brunstetter

ADVICE FOR IN THE KITCHEN

The meek shall eat and be satisfied;
they shall praise the LORD that seek him;
your heart shall live for ever.

PSALM 22:26

Meal Prepping

Know Your Food Sources

Know where your food comes from and know how to provide wholesome food for your table. Buy and eat the majority of your food grown locally.

Food for Health

Eat your food as close to its natural state as possible. Say no to processed foods with many preservatives.

Double Up

Double or triple a recipe and freeze the extra portions for quick future meals.

Do More with Your Egg Slicer

An egg slicer works great for slicing strawberries, mushrooms, boiled potatoes, cooked and peeled beets, and much more.

Don't Cry over Onions

Here are some great tear-free solutions for handling onions:

- Keep onions in the refrigerator. Warm onions easily release their fumes.
- Peel and cut onions under running water.
- Don't cut off the "bloom" end of the onion—where the fumes are stored.

Bean Gas

So that beans don't cause as much gas, discard the water you used to soak them in and use fresh water for cooking. Once they start cooking, leave the lid off. This will help remove toxins.

MIRIAM BYLER, SPARTANSBURG, PA

Dressing Recipe Idea

Bake dressing recipes in muffin tins. A pan of dressing muffins will bake at 350 degrees for 15 to 20 minutes and make perfectly portioned servings for your feast.

Rice

Rice will be fluffier and whiter if you add 1 teaspoon lemon juice to each quart of water.

Presoak Pasta for Fast Cooking

Soak your pasta in water in a sealed bag for a couple of hours or overnight. Drain and boil in fresh water. It will be fully cooked after 1 minute.

Pancake or Waffle Tip

When mixing batter, use a large 4-to-8-cup measuring bowl with a spout and handle. Then just pour the batter onto the griddle or waffle iron.

MALINDA M. GINGERICH, SPARTANSBURG, PA

Baking in Tins

Use a muffin pan for baking things like whole potatoes, whole apples, and stuffed green peppers.

An investment in knowledge always pays the best interest.

No-Mess Deviled Eggs

One no-mess method for deviling your eggs is to place your filling ingredients in a plastic bag. Massage the bag to mix; then cut a small hole in one corner of the bag. Squeeze the filling out of the bag and directly into the hollows of the egg whites.

Flavor Oops

Maybe you went a little overboard with your seasoning while cooking. For a quick fix to a dish that is too sweet or too salty, add a splash of vinegar. It will cut the sweet or saltiness without making the food taste vinegary.

Mrs. Daniel Wickey, Berne, IN

Soup

Always simmer soup. "Soup boiled is soup spoiled."

Malinda M. Gingerich, Spartansburg, PA

Soup Thickener

Instant mashed potatoes can be added to soup to thicken it. (To thin, add additional chicken broth.)

Greasy Food

When you see fat rise to the top of your casserole or noodles, lay a paper towel over the food to soak up the grease. Peel off paper towel and throw away.

Mary K. Bontrager, Middlebury, IN

Ice Cube Skimmer

When you find a skim of grease on the top of your soup or broth, place an ice cube on a slotted spoon and skim it over the grease. The grease will harden and stick to the spoon and the ice.

Stretching Soup

- When you need to stretch a pot of soup or casserole to feed a crowd, add a jar of beef or chicken broth.

Mrs. Henry J. Swartzentruber, Liberty, KY

- To thicken and stretch soups, add instant potato flakes to the right consistency.

Salomie E. Glick, Howard, PA

Frying Pan

- Heat frying pan before adding oil or butter to prevent sticking.

  Katie Yoder, Sugarcreek, OH

- Heat frying pan before adding oil or butter and sprinkle with salt to prevent food from sticking.

  Sadie Byler, Frazeysburg, OH

Splatters

To keep hot oil from splattering, sprinkle a little salt or flour in the pan before frying.

Bertha Schwartz, Monroe, IN

Saving Cooking Oil

To strain cooking oil after deep frying, put a paper coffee filter in a funnel and use to pour the oil back in the bottle to use again another time.

Heating Milk

Before heating milk in a saucepan, first rinse the pan with water, and it will keep the milk from scorching.

Nathan and Anna Fisher, Salisbury, PA

Creamier Pudding

For a richer, creamier pudding, use canned evaporated milk instead of regular whole milk.

A good beginning is half the job done.

Hot Chips

Put a tray of tortilla chips in a hot oven for just a few minutes. They will crisp up nicely, and your guests will love them warm.

Hot Drink Delight

For a wonderful addition to a hot drink, try cinnamon sticks. Even better, dip your cinnamon sticks in melted chocolate and let them dry before using them to stir your drink.

Punch Tip

Always chill juices or soda pop before adding to punch or other beverages.

Salomie E. Glick, Howard, PA

Slippery Cutting Board?

Keep your cutting board from sliding around on the countertop by cutting a piece of nonskid shelf liner to fit under the board.

Extra Counter Space

Counter space is often a precious commodity in a busy kitchen. For a quick and handy extra countertop, set up your ironing board and cover it with a plastic tablecloth.

From what we get we can make a living; what we give, however, makes a life.

VEGETABLES AND FRUITS

FRUIT AND VEGGIE WASH

½ cup apple cider vinegar   ½ cup water
½ cup lemon juice

Add ingredients to spray bottle and shake to combine. To use: spray liberally on fruits and vegetables; then rinse with cold water and prepare as usual. To store: refrigerate for up to a month.

It is important to wash pesticides and germs off your produce. This solution removes residues and has germ-killing properties.

SARAH ESH, KINZERS, PA

BANANAS

To ripen bananas fast, keep at room temperature. To ripen slowly, keep bananas in the refrigerator.

MIRIAM BYLER, SPARTANSBURG, PA

PEARS

To ripen green pears, place two or three in a brown bag, loosely close, and store at room temperature out of direct sunlight.

CRYSTAL ROPP, KALONA, IA

PEELING ORANGES

To peel an orange easily and to remove the rind in one piece to use for things like a bird feeder, a candle holder, or a serving dish, heat the orange in a bowl of very hot water for 3 to 4 minutes before peeling.

Juicing Lemons

- Allow lemons to warm to room temperature before you squeeze them to extract almost twice as much juice.

  Ruth Byler, Quaker City, OH

- Put lemons in a bowl of hot water before juicing and there will be twice as much juice.

  Salomie E. Glick, Howard, PA

- Freezing lemons and then thawing before juicing them will release more juice.

  Esther L. Miller, Fredericktown, OH

- Microwave a lemon for 10 to 20 seconds before trying to squeeze it.

Greens

Beet greens can be used in place of spinach.

Mary Stutzman, West Salem, OH

Lettuce Core

When cutting up a whole head of lettuce, use this nifty tip: To remove the core, give the head's core a whack on the countertop. Then give the core a twist, and it will come right out.

Husking Corn

To remove corn silk from corn on the cob, dampen a paper towel or terry cloth and brush downward on the cob. Every strand should come off.

Crystal Ropp, Kalona, IA

Rhubarb Tips

- To get that sour or tart taste out of rhubarb, wash and cut the stalks. Place in a stainless steel bowl and cover with boiling hot water. Let sit for an hour or more. Drain and use the rhubarb in your intended recipe. You can use the juice for a rhubarb drink by adding sugar and Kool-Aid drink mix of your choice. I always scald rhubarb before I use it, and nobody complains of it being too sour or tart or bitter. This is also a way to use less sugar!

  Lena Troyer, Redding, IA

- A little salt added to cooked rhubarb will help lessen the sugar needed to sweeten it.

  Emma Kurtz, Smicksburg, PA

Butter Water

- Put a tablespoon of butter in the water when cooking rice, dried beans, or macaroni to keep it from boiling over. Always run water over the rice, beans, or macaroni when done to get the starch out. Reheat over hot water if necessary.

  Emma Byler, New Wilmington, PA
  David and Laura Byler, New Castle, PA

- A little dab of butter in a kettle of potatoes will keep them from boiling over.

  Nathan and Anna Fisher, Salisbury, PA

Cooking Vegetables

Anything that grew underground (potatoes, carrots, beets, etc.), start cooking in cold water. Anything that grew above ground (peas, green beans, etc.), start cooking in boiling water. Corn on the cob is tastiest dropped into already boiling water for 3 minutes. It seals in the flavor and vitamins.

David and Laura Byler, New Castle, PA

How to Roast Vegetables

Set oven to 425 degrees. Chop vegetables. Firm vegetables like cauliflower, broccoli, potatoes, and carrots will take longer to cook than soft vegetables like summer squash, mushrooms, onion, and tomatoes, so either cut your firm vegetables smaller or add the soft vegetables later in the roasting process. Lightly toss vegetables in olive oil, salt, and pepper. Spread in a single layer on a baking sheet. Bake 30 to 40 minutes until tender.

Vegetable Peels

I hardly have vegetable peelings to throw away. Most things can be scrubbed well and cooked with the peels on. Yes, even potatoes. They make delicious mashed potatoes.

Mary Petersheim, Glenville, PA

Kindness is the oil that takes the friction out of life.

Before Roasting Potatoes

Put whole or large cut potatoes in boiling water for 6 to 10 minutes (depending on size) before roasting them in the oven. They cook faster and are less likely to dry out.

Tips for Prepping Potatoes

- Place whole potatoes in boiling water. Let them sit for a few minutes, and the skins will peel right off.
- Before peeling new potatoes, soak them in cold, salted water for 30 minutes. They will peel more easily and won't stain your hands.
- To slice potatoes with ease, first heat your knife in boiling water or over a gas flame.
- To keep your potatoes from turning black after peeling, soak them in cold water. Make sure they are fully covered. You can refrigerate them overnight this way. (Be sure to cover with plastic wrap.)
- When frying sliced or cubed potatoes, first sprinkle them lightly with flour so that they will have a golden coating when fried.

Tips for Improving Potatoes

- When you make mashed potatoes and it doesn't look like enough, add a little baking powder to fluff them up.

  S. Byler, Reynoldsville, PA

- When your potato casserole curdles, add a little baking soda. Then you almost can't notice it.

  S. Byler, Reynoldsville, PA

- To improve the taste of old potatoes, add a little sugar to the cooking water.
- A well-beaten egg white added to mashed potatoes will add to the taste and appearance of the dish.

How to Boil Potatoes

When making a potato salad or some potato casseroles, you first need to boil your potatoes. Choose an all-purpose potato with low starch like red, white, or Yukon Gold. Wash and peel. Cut to uniform size if needed—about 2 inches. Place potatoes in a pot and cover with cold water. Add a generous amount of salt— 1 tablespoon to a large pot. Bring water to a rolling boil. Cook 8 to 10 minutes until a fork easily pierces into the potatoes. Drain. If your recipe calls for grating the cooked potato, cook for a shorter time.

Squash Seeds

Scoop seeds from squash with an ice cream scoop.

Butternut Squash

When I cook butternut squash, I like to cook some sweet potato (yam) with it. Makes very tasty pie filling.

Adel Schmidt, Carlisle, KY

Cleaning Mushrooms

A soft makeup brush can be used in the kitchen to clean mushrooms and tender fruits.

Vegetable Tips

- Never soak vegetables after slicing, or they will lose much of their nutritional value.
- A lump of sugar added to water when cooking greens helps vegetables retain their fresh color.

Emma Byler, New Wilmington, PA

Smelly Cabbage

To prevent the odor of boiled cabbage from filling the house, put a little vinegar in the cooking water.

Caramelize Onions Quicker

Caramelize onions in a fraction of the time by adding baking soda.

Learn to be smart in the things that matter, give blessings to others, and let your love scatter.

Lettuce Salads

When preparing a salad with leafy greens and watery vegetables ahead of time, first place a small plate upside down in the bottom of the serving bowl. Any moisture that weeps from the vegetables will run under the plate, and the vegetables will stay fresh and crisp.

Lettuce

To perk up soggy lettuce, sprinkle it with a mixture of lemon juice and cold water.

BERTHA SCHWARTZ, MONROE, IN

Lettuce Rust

To prevent lettuce from rusting, line container with paper towels. For garden lettuce, paper towels can also be put between layers and over top to absorb moisture.

SHARON MILLER, AUBURN, KY

Celery

To keep celery crisp, stand it up in a pitcher of cold, salted water and refrigerate.

BARBARA TROYER, MILLERSBURG, OH

Limp Celery

When celery goes limp, slice a raw potato into a pan of cold water and place the celery in it for a few hours.

Chopping Garlic

When chopping garlic cloves, place a few drops of cooking oil on the edge of your paring knife before starting to chop. The minced pieces won't stick to the knife.

DAVID AND LAURA BYLER, NEW CASTLE, PA

Some small deed may help to brighten someone else's day.

MEATS

FRESH EGGS?

Are your eggs fresh? To determine freshness, immerse each egg in a pot of cool water. If it sinks, it is fresh; if it floats on the surface, throw it out.

TIPS ON HOW TO FRY AN EGG

Turn your stove on high. Put on a skillet and add a dollop of butter. Run out to the chicken house and fetch an egg. If the cluck doesn't put up too big of a fight and you don't trip over the dog, you should be on time to crack the egg into the skillet. Warning: if smoke alarm is going off, turn down the heat. After cracking the egg, pick out the pieces of shell. Salt lightly and pepper heavily. By now it should be ready to flip over easy. Repeat for each egg and enjoy.

MALINDA M. GINGERICH, SPARTANSBURG, PA

COOKING EGGS

- Use a funnel as an egg separator. Place the funnel over a glass and break the egg into the funnel. The egg white will pass through the funnel, leaving the yolk behind.
- If you get some yolk in your whites when separating eggs, moisten a cloth with cold water and touch to the yolk. It will cling to the cloth.
- When cooking eggs on the stove, always use low to moderate heat to keep them from becoming tough.
- When adding hot liquid to raw beaten eggs, do so just a little at a time so the egg doesn't cook and clump.

Boiled Eggs

To prevent eggs from cracking when boiling, dip in cold water before boiling.

SALOMIE E. GLICK, HOWARD, PA

How to Boil Eggs

Place eggs in pot and cover with cold water. Bring water to boil over high heat. When water reaches a hard boil, cover pot with lid and turn off heat. Let eggs cook for 8 to 10 minutes for soft yolk or 12 to 15 minutes for harder yolk. Drain off hot water and move eggs to a bowl of water and ice. Chill for 5 minutes. Drain. Let eggs reach room temperature, then peel.

Stretching Eggs

When making scrambled eggs and you are short on eggs, add milk or water to stretch them.

DANIEL STOLTZFUS, NOTTINGHAM, PA

Quick Thawing

- To thaw meat at room temperature, place it on a metal pan and turn occasionally. Metal conducts heat and speeds up the process.
- To thaw meat last minute for company or an unexpected event, put meat in cold water (not warm or hot). Cold water thaws faster and is better for the meat.

MARY K. BONTRAGER, MIDDLEBURY, IN

Golden Chicken

For golden-brown fried chicken, roll pieces in powdered milk instead of flour.

KATELYN ALBRECHT, MONTICELLO, KY

Chicken Coating

You can easily coat chicken by placing it, along with flour and seasoning mixture, into a brown lunch bag and shaking.

Tasty Sandwiches

Toast cheese sandwiches in a frying pan lightly greased with bacon fat for a delightful new flavor.

KATELYN ALBRECHT, MONTICELLO, KY

Grilling

When frying or grilling a hamburger, punch a small hole in the middle of it. It will get done quicker.

EMMA BYLER, NEW WILMINGTON, PA

Juicy Meat

A fork or knife should never be stuck into meat that is frying or grilling because it lets juices out. When done cooking, remove meat from heat and let rest before cutting into it so that the juices will have time to settle into the meat.

Juicy Hamburgers

For extra juicy and nutritious hamburgers, add ¼ cup evaporated milk per pound of meat before shaping it into patties.

DAVID AND LAURA BYLER, NEW CASTLE, PA

Uniform Hamburger Patties

To make uniform hamburger patties, find a jar lid of the desired size and wash it well. Pack the lid tightly with ground beef, smooth the top with a knife, turn it over, tap out the patty…and voilà! Beautifully shaped hamburgers!

Hamburger

I like to brown two packages of hamburger at one time. Then I have extra ready to use whenever I need in the next 4 days. (Can also be frozen for later.) This doesn't take any more time and makes for fewer dishes.

JOHN LLOYD AND SUSAN YODER, NEWAYGO, MI

Stretching Ground Meat

Ground meat can be stretched by adding quick oats and moistening them with tomato juice for less expensive burgers.

MRS. BETHANY MARTIN, HOMER CITY, PA

Every sunrise is a new message from God and every sunset His signature.

DAVID AND LAURA BYLER, NEW CASTLE, PA

Meat Ready?

If you have a hard time knowing if your meat is ready to turn, wait until you see juice on top. Then it is ready to turn.

Sadie Byler, Reynoldsville, PA

Meat Loaf

Meat loaf won't stick to the pan if you place a couple of bacon strips in the bottom of the pan before placing the meat loaf mixture in.

Adding Offal

I have found the best way to use beef heart is to grind it in with hamburger.

Arlene Bontrager, Middlebury, IN
Benjamin Yoder Jr., Narvon, PA

Seasoning

When seasoning meat, sprinkle some on the pan first, and then put the meat on top of the seasoning. It will stick right to your meat. Even saves time.

Sadie Byler, Reynoldsville, PA

Separating Bacon

To easily peel apart cold, uncooked bacon slices, roll the bacon up from the short end like a jelly roll. Unroll, flip over, and roll up again. Then the slices should separate without tearing.

Bacon

Bacon won't curl if dipped in cold water or sprinkled with flour before cooking.

Sadie Byler, Reynoldsville, PA

Bacon at the Ready

Cook a pound of bacon until done but not crisped. When cooled and drained of fat, cut or crumble the bacon and store it in a freezer container. It can then be added quickly to scrambled eggs, soup, a casserole, or a salad.

Bacon Grease

I save all my bacon grease and use it to fry eggs, potatoes, meats, and so forth. It can also be used to pop popcorn. If I have grease with lots of bacon bits in it, I scrape it into a separate jar and use it to make gravy.

Mrs. Chester Miller, Centerville, PA

Love is the master key that opens the gate of happiness.

What to Do with Leftovers?

Almost any kind of leftovers are good made into a soup by browning some butter in a kettle and adding the leftovers, stirring to warm and brown. Add enough milk to make enough servings for your family. Season with salt, pepper, and garlic powder. If you have Velveeta cheese, that would be a great addition. Be fearless! If you can't eat it, the dog probably can. But usually it turns out to be one of our favorite soups.

MRS. JOSEPH HOCHSTETLER, DANVILLE, OH

Free Soup

After cooking vegetables, pour any water and leftover vegetable pieces into a freezer container and freeze. When the container is full, add tomato juice and seasonings to create a money-saving "free" soup.

AMANDA SWARTZENTRUBER, DALTON, OH

How to Boil Chicken

Place chicken in a pot and cover with water. Add salt. Bring to a boil, cover, and cook over medium heat. Boneless chicken breasts should cook in 15 minutes. A whole bone-in chicken will take 45 to 60 minutes. Remove from water. Retain water to use as chicken broth. Cool chicken and remove any bones. (Bones can be cooked for bone broth.) Chop or shred chicken as called for in recipes.

How to Cook Bone Broth

Beef bones can be bought from the butcher or in grocery stores. Raw bones would benefit from being roasted in the oven at 350 degrees for 30 minutes before making broth. For poultry broth, save the bones from your chicken or turkey meals. Some meat on the bones is fine, but discard the skin. You can freeze bones until you have saved enough for a pot of broth. Place bones in a large pot or slow cooker and cover with water. Add 1 to 2 tablespoons apple cider vinegar to help release the minerals from the bones. You can also add some vegetables like onion, carrot, and celery. Bring to a boil; cook over low heat for about 1 hour for poultry and 2 or more hours for beef. Occasionally skim any foam from the top of the broth. Strain and use.

OTHER COOKING TIPS

HONEY

Store honey in the freezer to keep from crystallizing.

JOANN MILLER, FREDERICKTOWN, OH

CRYSTALLIZED HONEY

Crystallization is a natural process for raw honey, but it doesn't mean you have to throw it out. Place the jar of honey in a pan of warm water and stir the honey until the crystals dissolve. You can also microwave the honey for 30 seconds, stir, and repeat for another 30 seconds until the crystals have dissolved.

MEASURING HONEY WITH OIL

When using honey and oil in a recipe, measure the oil first in your measuring cup, then, when measuring honey in the same cup after emptying the oil, the honey will slide right out.

JUDITH ANNE MILLER, FREDERICKTOWN, OH

SALAD DRESSING TIP

To keep salad dressing like sweet-and-sour from separating and settling, try adding 1 teaspoon molasses.

MIRIAM BYLER, SPARTANSBURG, PA

THICK SALAD DRESSING

If your homemade salad dressing is too thick, just add water.

JOANN MILLER, FREDERICKTOWN, OH

CHEESE STORAGE

- To keep cheese from getting moldy, put a bay leaf or two into the package. It really works, and the bay leaf doesn't affect the flavor of the cheese.

  MALINDA M. GINGERICH, SPARTANSBURG, PA

- When you buy cheese in bulk and want to freeze leftovers after a gathering, put wax paper between each slice of cheese and freeze. When you want to thaw some, take it out of the freezer and put it in the refrigerator to thaw completely, and it won't be crumbly. The wax paper will let slices come apart easily.

  MARY K. BONTRAGER, MIDDLEBURY, IN

GRATING CHEESE

Freeze cheese for a short time so that grating is easier.

SALTSHAKER

Add uncooked rice to the saltshaker to keep the salt free flowing.

MENNO J. YODER FAMILY, BERLIN, PA
BERTHA SCHWARTZ, MONROE, IN

PUMPKIN SEEDS

Roast and eat your pumpkin seeds instead of throwing them out. They are a great remedy for expelling worms in people and animals.

KATIE HOOVER, EAST EARL, PA

REUSE CONTAINERS

Reuse a large spice container with the removable shaker shield or a grated Parmesan cheese container. Clean and dry well, then fill the container with flour and label it clearly. Use the flour to dust your greased baking pans. You can also use them for powdered sugar or a mixture of cinnamon and sugar.

REUSE BAGS

Keep store-bought bread bags to store homemade bread. Or cut them smaller for sandwich bags.

MIRIAM BYLER, SPARTANSBURG, PA

KID-FRIENDLY KITCHEN

Make your kitchen kid friendly by stocking up on plastic measuring cups, spoons, and mixing bowls. Consider buying from a yard sale or resale shop. Personalize them with a permanent marker. Your children will love using their own kitchen tools when they help you prepare snacks and meals.

Baking Tips

Step One

For the best possible outcome, start out with your eggs and butter at room temperature. Ingredients will blend easier and faster.

Baking Soda Test

To see if your baking soda is still active, put ½ teaspoon in ¼ cup hot water. If it bubbles vigorously, it is still good.

Miriam Byler, Spartansburg, PA

Taste of Baked Goods

If you dislike the taste of baking soda in baked goods, try using baking powder in place of the baking soda and dissolve it in a little sour milk before adding it to the recipe.

Menno J. Yoder family, Berlin, PA

Hard Butter

If you want to bake but your butter is too hard, grate it so that it mixes easier.

Mary Ann Byler, New Wilmington, PA

Quick Soft Butter

To soften butter, fill a bowl (one just larger than your stick of butter) with boiling water. Let stand a minute until the bowl is thoroughly heated. Then empty the bowl and immediately set the bowl upside down over the butter. In just a few minutes, the butter will be softened and ready to use.

Quick Soft Cream Cheese

To soften cream cheese fast, place unopened package in hot water.

Katie Yoder, Sugarcreek, OH

Egg Substitutes

- If you are short on eggs and need to bake, try 1 teaspoon cornstarch in ¼ cup water for each egg the recipe calls for.

Mrs. Christine Schmidt, Salem, IN

- When the recipe calls for several eggs and you are one egg short, substitute 1 teaspoon cornstarch in place of the missing egg.

David and Laura Byler, New Castle, PA

Hard Sugar

- If your sugar (white or brown) gets hard, add an apple to it. The apple should help keep it soft.

Mrs. Levi J. Stutzman, West Salem, OH

- Keep brown sugar soft by placing two to three large marshmallows in the canister with the brown sugar.

Powdered Sugar Substitute

Combine white sugar with a little cornstarch, about 1 tablespoon cornstarch to 1 cup sugar, in a blender. Blend until light and fluffy.

Mary Ann Byler, New Wilmington, PA

Fat-Free Baking

Did you can a lot of applesauce? Use it instead of oil in your cake recipes. Measure cup for cup. It's inexpensive, and you won't notice the difference in the cake.

Rachel Miller, Millersburg, OH

Mixing Tip

To prevent cold shortening or butter from sticking to the mixer beater, warm up the beaters in hot water before using.

MEASURING FLOUR

Flour packs down, so your method of measuring can have an effect on the outcome of your recipe. To start, use a spoon to stir the flour that has settled in your storage container. Then use the spoon to gently fill your measuring cup. Use a flat edge like a knife to level off the top of the cup's contents back into the flour bin. If the recipe calls for sifted flour, measure out the listed amount and then sift it. If you don't have a flour sifter, you can put the flour into a strainer and shake it into your mixing bowl. Or, you can also sift or fluff your flour with a whisk or fork.

CAKE FLOUR

If you don't have "cake" flour, measure the required amount using all-purpose flour. Remove 1 tablespoon for each cup and replace with 1 tablespoon cornstarch for each cup.

DRESS UP A BOXED CAKE MIX

To make a boxed cake taste homemade, substitute butter for oil and use milk instead of water. Add a teaspoon of vanilla and/or almond extract to white cakes for additional flavor.

To ease another's burden,
we need to help carry it.

Get Air Bubbles out of Cake Batter

- To keep your cake from getting holes, run a knife through the cake batter after you have finished mixing it. It will take out any air bubbles that could cause the cake to collapse.

  Martha Miller, Decatur, IN

- To ensure that your cakes don't have big air holes, fill the pans with batter and then lift and drop the pans several times until air bubbles rise to the surface and then pop.

Low and Slow Baking

Set oven temperatures lower for bigger cake pans. The cake will have to bake longer, but you won't run the risk of burning the outer edges by the time the middle is done.

Angel Food Cake

Follow these tips for easily making a great angel food cake.
- Have all ingredients at room temperature.
- Use cake flour only.
- Egg whites should contain no trace of egg yolk.
- Make sure the sugar is clean when beaten with egg whites. Any trace of flour could damage the meringue.
- Fold in flour and sugar mixture gently with spatula. Do not beat.
- Bake in ungreased tube pan and turn upside down to cool.
- Be careful not to overbake.

  Miriam Byler, Spartansburg, PA

Cake Tester

When you need to test the "doneness" of a cake or bread and you don't have a cake-testing tool, use an uncooked piece of spaghetti. It is long enough to test your deepest baked goods.

Too Much Sugar?

Many cookie recipes call for too much sugar. You can cut down on the sugar as much as half, particularly if you are using raisins, dates, chocolate chips, or some other sweet addition.

  Katie Zook, Apple Creek, OH

For Fluffy Cookies

For lighter, fluffier cookies, use vegetable shortening in place of butter.

Soft Cookies

For softer cakes and cookies, beat eggs well.

Mrs. Josep Miller, Navarre, OH

Perfectly Round Cookies

When slicing logs of refrigerated cookie dough, roll the dough every other cut so the bottom of the log doesn't flatten. Each cookie will be perfectly round.

Adding Fruit to Baked Goods

When adding fruit to sweet breads or cakes, always coat the fruit in flour before adding to the batter. This keeps the fruit from settling to the bottom.

You can give without loving, but you can't love without giving.

Butter Wrappers

Use empty butter wrappers to grease your cake pans or cookie sheets.

JUDITH ANNE MILLER, FREDERICKTOWN, OH

Greasing Pans

Slip your hand inside a sandwich bag and you have a perfect mitt for greasing your baking pans and casserole dishes.

EMMA BYLER, NEW WILMINGTON, PA

Dust Your Pans with Cocoa

If you prepare your pan with flour, you could end up with an unsightly white residue on your cake. Try dusting pans with cocoa instead of flour when you're baking a chocolate dessert.

Sugarcoat It

Try dusting your cake pans with regular sugar instead of flour. The mild, sweet coating on a cake is more appealing than lumpy flour.

Valentine-Shaped Cupcakes

Fill cupcake liner like usual. Then put a marble behind the liner in cupcake pan and bake. Results should look like hearts.

MARY ANN BYLER, NEW WILMINGTON, PA

There is one thing you will be sure to have help in doing, and that's minding your own business.

Using Cookie Cutters

Lightly coat cookie cutters—especially plastic ones—with oil spray to keep them from sticking to the cookie dough.

Nonstick Cake Trick

When you take a cake from the oven, place it on a water-soaked towel for a very short time. The cooled cake will turn out of the pan without sticking.

Cake Leveler

Need to trim off the top of your cake layers before stacking and filling? Use dental floss in a back-and-forth motion for a perfectly straight cut.

Frosting Cleanly

To prevent cake from peeling while frosting, sprinkle with powdered sugar before frosting.

RHODA MILLER, DECATUR, IN

Glittery Frosting

Add color and sparkle to white frosting by sprinkling lightly with dry gelatin powder of your choice of color and flavor.

Black Frosting

For black frosting, you can add blue food coloring to chocolate frosting.

Peanut Butter in Frosting

Peanut butter is a flavorful substitute for butter or margarine in powdered sugar–based frostings. Use the same amount as you would butter. It adds a nutty flavor.

DAVID AND LAURA BYLER, NEW CASTLE, PA

Cake Decorating

To keep cake plate clean while frosting a cake, slide 6-inch strips of wax paper under each side of the cake. Once the cake is frosted and frosting is set, pull the strips away, leaving a clean plate.

EMMA BYLER, NEW WILMINGTON, PA

FROSTING BAG TIP

Need to fill a frosting bag? Place it in a tall cup and fold the edges down.

LEFTOVER FROSTING

When baking, if I have leftover frosting, I put it between two graham crackers. The children love this treat.

MRS. CHESTER MILLER, CENTERVILLE, PA

CHOCOLATE CURLS

To make chocolate curls, use a block of chocolate at room temperature. Hold it in your hands for a while to warm it up. Once the chocolate is the proper temperature, run a vegetable peeler across the side of the bar, using moderate pressure, to produce curls. If you've never made chocolate curls before, you'll have to practice a few times to get it right; but once you see the end result, you'll agree that it's worth the extra work.

COVERING A CAKE

Have you ever created a mess when you've tried to put a cover over a frosted cake? When you don't have a raised lid for your cake pan, lay a paper towel over the top instead. The frosting will stick at first, but soon the oils in the frosting will soak into the towel, and when you are ready to remove the paper towel, your frosting won't be pulled from the cake.

There is no teaching to compare with example.

Salvaging Burned Cookies or Toast

Use a handheld grater or zester to shave the char from slightly burned cookies or toast.

Hard Cookies

- If your cookies get hard, put a piece of bread in your cookie container. Even if the cookies are hardened, the bread will soften them. Also try this on hardened brown sugar.

    Miriam Byler, Spartansburg, PA

- Placing several pieces of sliced bread in a container of hard cookies will help to soften them.

    Nathan and Anna Fisher, Salisbury, PA

Cooling Cookies

When baking cookies and you run out of space on your cooling racks, use newspaper. Lay out three sheets thick. Put cookies on to cool. This works well for me when I have lots of cookies to bake for church. When done, just roll up the newspaper for quick and easy cleanup.

    Mary K. Bontrager, Middlebury, IN

Repurposed Racks

Old metal racks from worn-out refrigerators and ovens make good cooling racks for cookies and other baked goods. Their large size is great for holiday baking sprees.

Mailing Cookies

When preparing cookies to mail, use plastic wrap to package cookies in pairs, back to back. Choose a soft-variety cookie, as crisp cookies tend to crumble in transit. Empty potato chip cans make good shipping containers.

Baking Products That Last

Baking products can be expensive, and you don't want anything to go to waste. If you don't bake very often or like to buy your baking ingredients in bulk, you can keep many products like baking chocolate, baking chips, flour, nuts, dried fruits, butter, marshmallows, and cream cheese in the freezer until you are ready to use them.

No-Stick Dough

To keep dough from sticking to your rolling pin, try using nylon. Take a clean, never-worn knee-high stocking and cut off the toe. Slide the nylon over your rolling pin. The nylon helps hold an even layer of flour on the pin so you can easily flatten moist dough.

PIECRUST TIPS

- For the flakiest possible crust, use ice-cold water. Add a pinch of salt for better taste.
- Dusting pie pan with flour before lining with pie dough will prevent piecrust from sticking during baking.
- To prevent soggy piecrust, first brush the pie shell with egg white and then add the filling. The egg white creates a barrier between the dough and the filling.
- To prevent juices from running out of fruit pies, make a cone of parchment paper and insert the small end into the center vent of the piecrust. Be sure the cone is at least 2 inches above the piecrust to allow for juice bubbling during baking.

FLAKY PIE CRUST

Add a teaspoon of vinegar to pie dough and use milk instead of water for a flaky crust.

SADIE BYLER, FRAZEYSBURG, OH

BROWNED PIE CRUST

- To brown pie crust, use a small pastry brush to coat the piecrust with beaten egg before baking the pie.

MENNO J. YODER FAMILY, BERLIN, PA

- Brush beaten egg mixed with a little white sugar on top of piecrust to brown nicely.

MRS. JOSEP MILLER, NAVARRE, OH

PREBAKED PIE CRUST

To prevent an unfilled piecrust from puffing up during baking, prick the unbaked pastry in the pie pan before baking. This helps the steam to escape during baking.

MALINDA M. GINGERICH, SPARTANSBURG, PA

CRUST PROTECTOR

- When baking a pie, the crust will get brown before the pie is done. Take a foil pie pan and cut a 6-inch circle out of the middle. Then put the pan upside down over your baking pie. The pie will finish baking, but the crust will not get overdone.

MARY K. BONTRAGER, MIDDLEBURY, IN

- To prevent your piecrust edges from getting too brown, cover the edge with a strip of aluminum foil.

MALINDA M. GINGERICH, SPARTANSBURG, PA

Meringue

Mix 1 teaspoon cornstarch for each egg white with the sugar and a pinch of cream of tartar for a nice meringue.

SADIE BYLER, FRAZEYSBURG, OH

Making Custard

When making egg custard, always heat the milk to the boiling point. It keeps the undercrust crisp.

SALOMIE E. GLICK, HOWARD, PA

Whole Wheat Bread

To make soft whole wheat bread without adding white flour, add a crushed vitamin C tablet to the dough. One tablet for every three loaves.

RUTH BYLER, QUAKER CITY, OH

Baking Bread

- When baking bread, bake for 10 minute, then move the pans around in the oven for even loaves.

KATIE YODER, SUGARCREEK, OH

- When bread is baking, place a small pan of water in the oven to keep the crust from getting too hard.

Experience is something you don't get until after you need it.

Basic Breadmaking Directions and Tips

If you follow this, your bread should be perfect!

After mixing ingredients as directed in your recipe, grease hands and knead dough vigorously about 5 to 10 minutes or until dough squeaks. You may wish to turn dough out on floured tabletop for kneading. Place dough in greased bowl and grease top of dough. Cover and set in warm place away from drafts. Let rise until doubled. Knead lightly to release air bubbles. Again, grease bowl and top of dough. Repeat this procedure until dough has risen two or three times (whatever the recipe calls for).

Divide dough into given portions and form into loaves. Bang each loaf hard with the palm of your hand to get rid of air bubbles. Place in greased loaf pans with smooth side of dough up. Brush grease/butter over top of each loaf and prick deeply with fork to release air bubbles. Let rise until doubled in size. Bake as directed in your recipe. Grease top of loaf again immediately after removing from oven. Remove from pans and cool on rack.

Sealing bread in plastic bags before it is completely cooled will keep crust soft.

Malinda M. Gingerich, Spartansburg, PA

Revive Bread

To freshen dry bread, wrap it in a damp towel and place it in the refrigerator for 24 hours. Remove towel and heat the bread in the oven for a few minutes.

Sadie Byler, Frazeysburg, OH

Ask God to bless your food, but don't expect Him to make your bread.

CLEANUP TIPS

QUICK SPILL PICKUP!

When measuring dry ingredients, especially if children are helping, chances are you'll wind up with a mess on your countertop. Do your measuring over a paper plate or a sheet of wax paper. Spills can then be picked up easily and returned to the canister.

GLOVES

Keep disposable gloves in the kitchen for mixing meat loaf and meatballs.

COOKBOOK

To keep a cookbook clean, open to the page you need, then slip the book into a large plastic storage bag.

NO DRIPS

Grease the spout of a pitcher of milk, cream, gravy, and the like with butter to prevent drips.

BLENDER CLEANUP

For a quick blender cleanup, fill a third of the blender with hot water. Add a drop of dish detergent. Cover and turn on for a few seconds. Rinse and dry.

EASY PAN CLEANUP

- When you empty pots of food, put some hot water in the pot and replace the lid tightly. Set aside. Your pots will be much easier to clean.
- For burned-on food in a pan, while pan is still warm, sprinkle with about a teaspoon of baking soda and cover with water. Let sit until cool, and cleaning should be easy.

Baking Soda Paste

Cleaning up a greasy mess doesn't have to be a chore if you use this little trick: Sprinkle a generous amount of baking soda into your pan when you are done cooking; add a bit of water and blend to form a paste. Let your pan stand while you and your family enjoy a meal together. When you are ready to wash your pan, it will clean up fast. You won't believe the shine! (This little cleaning tip also works wonders on the stove top.)

Quick and Easy Flour Cleanup

Before washing a bowl that had flour in it, first rinse in cold water. Hot water causes flour to gel and become harder to wash away.

Cleaning Egg

If raw egg spills on the countertop or floor, don't try to wipe with a rag as it will just smear it around. Cover it thickly with salt and let dry. Then it will sweep up easily.

Cast Iron

Never scrub a cast iron kettle or skillet with a scouring pad. The protective coating will be removed and food will stick.

Susie Kinsinger, Fredericktown, OH

Smelly Cutting Board

Bleach your cutting board with lemon juice. It will keep the bad smells away. Baking soda works too. Just rub it in.

Katelyn Albrecht, Monticello, KY

Hand Odor

- Remove onion and garlic odors from hands by rubbing fingers with salt moistened with vinegar.
- If you have smelly hands from garlic, onion, fish, or other food item, wash them with toothpaste and very warm water.

Nora Miller, Millersburg, OH
David and Laura Byler, New Castle, PA

Refrigerator Odors

To remove odors from the refrigerator, mix dry mustard with cold water until pasty and set uncovered dish in the refrigerator overnight.

Stain Preventer

Protect plastic storage containers from unsightly tomato stains by spraying them with cooking oil before filling them.

Leftovers

If you have leftovers for just one or two servings, put in a freezer bag and freeze for a handy lunch box meal.

Nora Miller, Millersburg, OH

Leftover Pancakes

Freeze leftover pancakes or pieces of french toast with pieces of wax paper between each. Good for a quick breakfast that can be heated in the toaster or microwave.

Cleaning Baking Dishes

Baking dishes that have been browned from use can be soaked in a strong solution of Borax in water to remove the stains.

Any housewife, no matter how large her family, can always get some time alone by doing the dishes.

David and Laura Byler, New Castle, PA

Tips for Hosting Guests

Hospitality

Have a guest room (or a plan) always ready to receive a visitor or a friend in need. Hospitality is an often overlooked act of love.

Prep Work

When I'm expecting company, I like to prepare food ahead.

- Mix meat loaf or hamburger patties ahead. They can be stored in the refrigerator 2 to 3 days.
- Pork and beans made the day before and warmed in the oven before serving have a wonderful flavor.
- Salads can be prepared early morning of the day of the dinner.
- For pies, make crusts up to 2 weeks ahead, freeze, and thaw the day before filling and baking.
- Pie fillings can be prepared 2 days before filling crust and baking.

Susie Kinsinger, Fredericktown, OH

Serving Warm Rolls

To help keep rolls or buns warm at the table, heat up a ceramic tile in the oven while they are baking. Place the warm tile in the bottom of the bread basket and place the rolls on top. Cover with a cloth.

Hot Gravy

Use a thermal coffee carafe or two to serve gravy at large dinners like Thanksgiving or Christmas or potlucks. Gravy never gets to people fast enough when so many dishes are making their way around. The carafe holds a lot of gravy and keeps it hot at the table.

Sleepy Guests

If you are burning your fireplace as you entertain several people in the room, crack a window somewhere. Gas log and wood fires use up the oxygen in your room over several hours and can make it a little harder to breathe and stay awake.

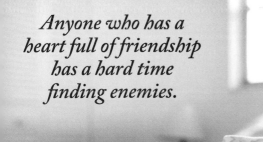

Anyone who has a heart full of friendship has a hard time finding enemies.

Tips for Transporting Food

- To keep food cold if you don't have ice packs, put a gallon-sized zipper bag inside another bag of the same size. Fill inside bag with ice. Squeeze out air and seal both bags. Put inside your carrier before adding your cold dish.

  MARY K. BONTRAGER, MIDDLEBURY, IN

- Save clean pizza boxes to transport pies, cookies, and rolls to bake sales, auctions, or other events.

  EMMA JO HOCHSTETLER, NAPPANEE, IN

- A good way to transport hot or cold food is to fold a bath towel so it fits in the bottom of an ice chest. Set your pot, roaster, or whatever is hot on the towel. Fold another towel and lay it on top and close the chest tightly. The hot food will stay hot! If you are taking a frozen dish, do the same with towels in an ice chest. You can also add dry ice packs. We've had it happen that the dish is still so frozen hard that it needs to sit awhile before it can be served.

  MATTIE PETERSHEIM, JUNCTION CITY, OH

- I like to use a clean bath towel or a clean blanket to wrap hot roasters in to keep the food from cooling.

  ANNA M. YODER, MERCER, MO

- Wrap wet newspaper around ice cream containers. It may freeze on in places. Cover with more dry newspaper. The ice cream should not melt.

  ANNA M. YODER, MERCER, MO

- Put your hot meat in an ice chest lined with aluminum foil. It will stay hot for hours.

  AMANDA ZEHR, SPENCERVILLE, IN

- Before taking dishes and utensils to gatherings, mark them with nail polish. It won't wash off but can be removed later with fingernail polish remover.
- Freeze bottles of water to use as cooler ice packs and as dead space filler to make your freezer run more efficiently.

TIPS FOR PICNICS

- If you are eating outside, lay tea leaves around on the tables and between food dishes to keep the flies away.
- When you are having a cookout or picnic and don't have tablecloth clips, take wide-mouth canning jar flat lids and bend about 1½ inches from each side so it looks like a D. Slide over side of table over the cloth.

MARY K. BONTRAGER, MIDDLEBURY, IN

There's no telling how far a kind look or deed will travel.

BASIC RECIPES

BREAD CRUMBS

To make your own bread crumbs: Crumble dry or stale bread onto cookie sheets and dry on woodstove or in gas stove with pilot on. Once bread is dry, you can grind it or blend it if you have a blender. Use to coat and fry eggplant or zucchini. Season and use for chicken or whatever you wish.

DAVID AND MALINDA BEILER, WATSONTOWN, PA

ITALIAN BREAD CUBES

We like to use old bread for this as it makes it tasty again. Heat skillet and add plenty of butter, a good sprinkle of Italian seasoning, parsley flakes, and garlic powder. Add bread cubes and toast until slightly browned. Serve with gravy or soup. We love these seasonings, but you can use your favorites. Be creative!

LEVI AND MARY MILLER, JUNCTION CITY, OH

HERB SALT

1 cup dried and ground herbs (e.g., combination of alfalfa, clove, dandelion, celery leaves, chives, onion, garlic)	1 cup salt 1 cup water

Use herbs of your choice. Mix herbs, salt, and water and let stand for one week. Put on cookie sheet and dry thoroughly. Crumble fine with rolling pin.

EMMA BEILER, DELTA, PA

Taco Seasoning

9 teaspoons chili powder
9 teaspoons paprika
13½ teaspoons cumin
18 teaspoons parsley flakes

9 teaspoons onion powder
4½ teaspoons garlic salt
4½ teaspoons oregano

Mix and store in airtight container. Seven teaspoons mix equal one store-bought package.

LINDA BURKHOLDER, FRESNO, OH

Seasoned Salt

1 cup salt
2 tablespoons celery seed
2 tablespoons garlic salt
2 tablespoons paprika

2 teaspoons dry mustard
2 teaspoons onion powder
2 teaspoons pepper

Place all ingredients in blender. Blend well or mix and store in tight container.

EMMA BYLER, NEW WILMINGTON, PA

Homemade Garlic or Onion Powder

Peel garlic or onion and slice to no more than ¼ inch thick. Place in single layer on cookie sheet. Set oven to lowest temperature (below 180 degrees) and dry until brittle, stirring occasionally to prevent any pieces from getting too dark. Grind to powder. Return to oven until all dampness is out. Store in airtight container.

NATHAN AND ANNA FISHER, SALISBURY, PA

Hidden Valley Ranch Mix Copycat

5 tablespoons dried minced onion
7 tablespoons parsley flakes

4 teaspoons dried minced garlic
1 teaspoon garlic powder

Combine ingredients and store in airtight container. For dressing: combine 2 tablespoons mix with 1 cup homemade mayonnaise and 1 cup sour cream. For dip: combine 2 tablespoons mix with 2 cups sour cream.

SARAH STUTZMAN, HOMER, MI

Aluminum-Free Baking Powder

½ cup cream of tartar
¼ cup cornstarch

¼ cup baking soda

Mix together and store in airtight container.

TOBY AND RACHEL HERTZLER, CHARLOTTE COURT HOUSE, VA
SARAH STUTZMAN, HOMER, MI

Gluten-Free Cookie Flour Mix

2 cups white rice flour
1 cup tapioca starch
1½ cups oat flour

¼ cup potato starch or potato flour
¼ cup coconut flour

Combine all ingredients. Store in airtight container.

JULIA TROYER, FREDERICKSBURG, OH

Homemade Pan Coating

Make your own pan coating: Mix equal parts shortening, vegetable oil, and flour. Mix thoroughly and store, covered, in refrigerator. Use at room temperature to coat baking pans instead of spray or other method. It works wonders!

Sweetened Condensed Milk

1 cup evaporated cane sugar
2 cups milk

4 teaspoons cornstarch

In saucepan, combine sugar, milk, and cornstarch and bring to a boil. Boil for 5 to 7 minutes. Yield: 14 ounces.

HANNAH HOCHSTETTLER, CENTREVILLE, MI

If you have not often felt the joy of doing a kindly act, you have neglected much, and mostly yourself.

Homemade "Honey"

5 pounds sugar	1 teaspoon alum
3 cups water	85 red clover blossoms

In saucepan, bring sugar and water to a boil. Boil until water is clear (about 1 minute). Add alum and boil for 2 minutes. Remove from heat. Add clover blossoms. Let stand 10 minutes. Strain. Good on things like pancakes.

Anna Hershberger, Fredericksburg, OH

Maple Syrup

2 cups brown sugar	½ cup butter
2 cups water	Maple flavoring

Combine all ingredients and bring to a boil.

Mrs. Josep Miller, Navarre, OH

Corn Syrup Substitute

1 cup sugar	1 cup water
½ teaspoon white vinegar	¼ teaspoon salt

Boil all ingredients for 5 to 10 minutes. Store in glass jar.

Mrs. Reuben (Anna) Lapp, Rockville, IN

Homemade Karo Syrup

5 pounds sugar	½ to 1 teaspoon alum
3 cups water	(the size of a cherry)

In stockpot, combine sugar and water and cook until clear. Add alum. Cook for 2 minutes. Remove from heat and cover. Do not remove lid until the next day (about 24 hours later). The syrup will not get sugary and is nice and thick. If you want a thinner syrup, add water.

Emma Kurtz, Smicksburg, PA

Homemade Mayonnaise

1 fresh egg
½ teaspoon salt
½ teaspoon dry mustard
¼ teaspoon paprika

1 tablespoon vinegar
1 tablespoon lemon juice
1 cup light olive oil

Blend egg, salt, dry mustard, paprika, vinegar, and lemon juice. Very slowly add oil.

RACHEL MILLER, MILLERSBURG, OH
SARAH STUTZMAN, HOMER, MI

Homemade Mustard

5 cups water
5 cups sugar
5 eggs
2½ cups vinegar
6 heaping tablespoons flour

5 heaping tablespoons
 dry mustard
1 teaspoon turmeric
¾ teaspoon salt

Bring water to a boil. Beat all other ingredients together to make a paste. Add paste to boiling water. Boil until thick, stirring constantly, about 10 minutes.

CHARLENE KUEPFER, MILVERTON, ONTARIO, CANADA

A smile is a very powerful weapon; you can even break ice with it.

Cheese Sauce

2 tablespoons butter
2 tablespoons flour
2 cups milk, divided

1 cup diced Velveeta cheese
½ teaspoon salt

In saucepan, melt butter. Stir in flour and 1 cup milk. Stir to remove lumps and cook for a couple of minutes to thicken. Add remaining 1 cup milk, cheese, and salt, stirring until cheese is melted.

Mrs. Reuben (Martha) Byler, Atlantic, PA

How to Make a White Sauce

A white sauce is a basic component to many cream soups, casseroles, gravies, or pasta sauces. In saucepan over medium heat, melt 2 tablespoons butter. Add 2 tablespoons flour and cook until incorporated. Slowly pour in 1 cup milk, stirring or whisking constantly as it cooks and thickens.

Old-Fashioned Skillet Gravy

After you are done frying meat, add 2 tablespoons flour to the skillet you used and fry until browned. Stir constantly so it won't scorch. Slowly add hot water, stirring constantly until desired thickness. Season with salt and pepper. *Nothing is wasted!*

John Lloyd and Susan Yoder, Newaygo, MI

Homemade Cream Soup

3 tablespoons butter, melted
3 tablespoons flour
¼ teaspoon salt
1 cup milk

Optional additions (1 to 2 cups total): cheese, chopped celery, chopped onion, diced mushrooms, etc.

Mix all together in saucepan and cook until thickened. Use in place of 1 can condensed cream soup.

Mary Petersheim, Apple Creek, OH

Easy Sour Cream

2 cups heavy cream

2 tablespoons plain yogurt

Stir together cream and yogurt. Set at room temperature for 12 to 15 hours or until desired thickness. Will thicken if chilled.

Katie Petersheim, Lakeview, MI

Almond Milk

1 cup raw almonds
2 cups water, plus additional
   water for soaking

Honey to taste

Place almonds in bowl and cover with water. Cover and let stand overnight. Drain and rinse under cool water. Discard water. Put mushy almonds and 2 cups water into blender. Pulse for 2 minutes to break up almonds, then blend thoroughly for 2 minutes. Strain through cheesecloth. Press all almond milk from meal. If sweetener is desired, add honey. Refrigerate.

How to Whip Cream

Pour cold heavy whipping cream into deep bowl. Whisk by hand or use electric mixer until peaks begin to form as cream stiffens. Add a little sugar and a dash of vanilla. Serve chilled.

Cool Whip Substitute

2 cups heavy cream
1 tablespoon instant Clear Jel

¼ cup sugar

Whip cream until soft peaks form. Mix Clear Jel and sugar. Sprinkle over cream. Whip until desired texture.

Sarah Stutzman, Homer, MI

Simple Good Frosting or Candy

⅓ cup warm coconut oil
⅓ cup maple syrup

⅓ cup cocoa powder
10 drops peppermint oil

Put all ingredients in blender and blend until smooth. Use to frost chocolate cake or pour onto parchment paper, chill, and cut into small squares for candies.

Rachel Miller, Millersburg, OH

Simple Chocolate Syrup

1 cup maple syrup   ½ cup cocoa powder

Combine ingredients. Use to make chocolate milk or to top ice cream.

KATIE GINGERICH, DALTON, OH

Nonstick Cooking Spray

Liquid lecithin
Olive oil

Mix equal parts liquid lecithin and olive oil. Brush into your cookware and bakeware for nonstick cooking. Very little is needed. Note: Liquid lecithin can be purchased at most health food stores and some bulk food stores.

MIRIAM MILLER, STANFORD, KY

Don't ask God for what you think is good; ask Him for what He thinks is good for you.

Homemade Lard

Pork fat or beef tallow

Cut all fat into 1-inch cubes. Put into stainless steel canning pot. Do not fill more than half full so it doesn't boil over. Heat and boil until pieces stay together when pressed against side of canner. Turn off heat. Scoop pieces out with stainless steel strainer or spoon. Keep these to put in your suet feeder for the birds or give to the chickens in winter. Let the liquid fat cool awhile; then pour into glass jars with canning lids. It will keep a long time without sealing. Use for bird suet, homemade laundry soap, fried food, baking, and so on.

Caution: Fat is a lot hotter than water. Keep children away. It takes a long time to cool, even when off heat. Put salt on grease fires, not water, because water will explode and spread fire. If fat starts smoking, immediately turn off heat as it can catch fire.

MIRIAM BYLER, SPARTANSBURG, PA

Chicken Fat (Schmaltz)

Place fat pieces in saucepan. Boil slowly uncovered. When reduced to liquid, strain. Pour into glass jars. Refrigerate. Can be used for making popcorn or frying.

ARLENE BONTRAGER, MIDDLEBURY, IN

Make Your Own Vinegar

Pour freshly made cider (with tart apples is best) in amount of your choice into a 5-gallon bucket. Cover bucket with clean, dry cloth, and rubber band in place. Leave in warm place for a few weeks, then move to cellar for 3 to 6 months. It makes its own mother, and when it goes down to the bottom and becomes clearer, it is ready to use. You can also taste it to find out if it's ready. It can be used for baking or canning. Dilute it with water for canning as it is stronger than white vinegar.

MRS. LIZZIE N. CHRISTNER, BERNE, IN

Natural Food Colorings

- Blue: Boil ½ cup water and ½ cup blueberries for 5 minutes. Strain and store in jar in refrigerator. Makes about 1½ cups.
- Brown: Carob powder or syrup can be used to flavor or color frosting.
- Green: Boil spinach leaves or alfalfa tea and ½ cup water for 5 minutes. Strain and store in jar in refrigerator. Makes 1 cup.
- Orange: Place carrots in blender and grind into small pieces. Add ¼ cup water and blend until smooth. Strain and store in jar in refrigerator. Makes ¼ cup.
- Red: Boil 2 cups beets and ¾ cup water for 5 minutes. Strain and store in jar in refrigerator. Use sparingly. Icing will pick up red beet flavor. Makes 1 cup.
- Yellow: Add 1 teaspoon saffron to boiling water. Boil for 5 minutes. Strain and store in jar in refrigerator. Makes 1 cup.
- Peach: Mix 1 part red and 1 part yellow colorings. Strain and store in jar in refrigerator.

Note: Colorings may be frozen.

Hannah Beiler, Peach Bottom, PA

No person can do everything,
but each one can do something.

HANDY CHARTS

DID YOU KNOW?

- A Tupperware Fix-n-Mix bowl holds 50 to 60 cookies.
- There are 2 cups of peanut butter in an 18-ounce jar.
- A 12-ounce bag of chocolate chips equals 2 cups.
- A half cup of Clear Jel will thicken 1 quart of liquid.

KATIE YODER, SUGARCREEK, OH

COMMON EQUIVALENTS

APPLES: 1 pound = about 3 medium

BEANS: 1 cup dry = 2 to 2½ cups cooked

BUTTER: 1 stick = 8 tablespoons OR 4 ounces OR ½ cup

CARROT: 1 medium = ½ cup chopped, shredded, or sliced

CHEESE: 4 ounces = 1 cup shredded

CHOCOLATE CHIPS: 6 ounces = 1 cup

EGG WHITE: 1 large = about 2 tablespoons

EGG YOLK: 1 large = about 1½ tablespoons

GELATIN: 1 envelope unflavored = 2½ teaspoons

GRAHAM CRACKERS: 1 cup crumbs = 7 whole crackers

HEAVY CREAM: 1 cup = 1¾ to 2 cups whipped cream

LEMON: 1 medium = 2 teaspoons zest and 3 tablespoons juice

LIME: 1 medium = 1½ teaspoons zest and 2 tablespoons juice

MUSHROOMS: 8 ounces = 3 cups chopped or sliced

Onion: 1 medium = ½ cup chopped

Orange: 1 medium = 1 tablespoon zest and ⅓ cup juice

Pepper, bell: 1 medium = ¾ cup chopped

Popcorn: ¼ cup unpopped = about 4 cups popped

Potatoes: 1 pound = about 3 medium OR 2¾ cups peeled and cubed OR 2 cups mashed

Rice: 1 cup uncooked = 3 cups cooked

Tomato: 1 medium = ½ cup peeled, seeded, and chopped

Common Substitutions

Baking powder: 1 teaspoon = ½ teaspoon cream of tartar plus ¼ teaspoon baking soda

Baking soda: 1 teaspoon = 4 teaspoons baking powder

Bread crumbs, dry: ¼ cup = ¼ cup cracker crumbs OR ¼ cup cornflake crumbs OR 1 cup ground oats

Broth: 1 cup = 1 teaspoon or 1 cube instant beef or chicken bouillon plus 1 cup hot water

Butter: 1 cup = 1 cup margarine OR 1 cup shortening or lard plus ¼ teaspoon salt

Buttermilk: 1 cup = 1 tablespoon lemon juice or vinegar plus enough milk to make 1 cup (let stand 5 minutes before using) OR ⅔ cup plain yogurt plus ⅓ cup water OR ½ cup plain yogurt or sour cream plus ½ cup milk

Chocolate, unsweetened: 1 ounce = 3 tablespoons unsweetened cocoa powder plus 1 tablespoon oil or melted shortening

Cornstarch: 1 teaspoon = 1 tablespoon flour OR 1 teaspoon arrowroot starch

Corn syrup: 1 cup = 1¼ cups sugar plus ⅓ cup water OR 1 cup honey

Cream cheese: 1 cup = 1 cup pureed cottage cheese OR 1 cup plain yogurt, strained overnight through cheesecloth

Cream of tartar: 1 teaspoon = 2 teaspoons lemon juice or vinegar

Garlic: 1 clove = ½ teaspoon minced bottled garlic OR ⅛ teaspoon garlic powder

Half-and-half or light cream: 1 cup = 1 tablespoon melted butter plus enough whole milk to make 1 cup OR 1 tablespoon water plus enough heavy cream to make 1 cup

Heavy cream: 1 cup = ¾ cup milk plus ¼ cup melted butter (Note: will not whip)

Herbs, fresh: 1 tablespoon = ½ to 1 teaspoon dried herbs OR ½ teaspoon ground herbs

Honey: 1 cup = 1¼ cups sugar plus ⅓ cup water OR 1 cup corn syrup

KETCHUP: 1 cup = ½ cup tomato sauce, 2 tablespoons sugar, 1 tablespoon vinegar, and 1 teaspoon ground cloves

LARD: 1 cup = 1 cup shortening or butter

LEMON JUICE: 1 teaspoon = ½ teaspoon vinegar OR 1 teaspoon lime juice

MAYONNAISE: 1 cup = 1 cup sour cream or plain yogurt

MILK: dairy, 1 cup = 1 cup light coconut, almond, or soy milk OR ⅔ cup evaporated milk plus ⅓ cup water OR ½ cup heavy cream and ½ cup water OR ¼ cup dry milk powder plus 1 cup water

MOLASSES: 1 cup = 1 cup honey OR ¾ cup brown sugar plus 1 teaspoon cream of tartar

MUSTARD, DRY: 1 teaspoon = 1 tablespoon prepared mustard

MUSTARD, PREPARED: 1 tablespoon = 1 tablespoon dry mustard, 1 teaspoon vinegar, 1 teaspoon water, and 1 teaspoon sugar

ONION, CHOPPED: ½ cup = 2 tablespoons dry minced onion OR ½ teaspoon onion powder

PERMA-FLO STARCH: 1 tablespoon = 1 tablespoon arrowroot, cornstarch, Clear Jel, or Therm-flo OR 3 tablespoons flour

POWDERED SUGAR: Place a scoop of granulated sugar into spice grinder or food processor. Pulverize into fluffy white powdered sugar.

SHORTENING: 1 cup = 1 cup lard or butter

SOUR CREAM: 1 cup = 1 cup plain yogurt

SOUR MILK: 1 cup = 1 tablespoon vinegar plus enough milk to make 1 cup

SOY SAUCE: ½ cup = ¼ cup Worcestershire sauce plus 1 tablespoon water

SUGAR, BROWN: 1 cup packed = 1 cup sugar plus 2 tablespoons molasses

SUGAR, WHITE: 1 cup = 1 cup packed light brown sugar OR 2 cups sifted powdered sugar

SWEETENED CONDENSED MILK: 1 (14 ounce) can = ¾ cup sugar plus ½ cup water and 1⅛ cup dry powdered milk; bring to a boil and cook about 20 minutes, stirring often, until thickened

TOMATO JUICE: 1 cup = ½ cup tomato sauce plus ½ cup water

TOMATO SAUCE: 2 cups = ¾ cup tomato paste plus 1 cup water

VANILLA BEAN: 1 whole = 2 teaspoons vanilla extract

VEGETABLE OIL FOR BAKING: 1 cup = 1 cup applesauce

VINEGAR: 1 teaspoon = 1 teaspoon lemon juice

Candy Cooking Terminology

Thread (230 degrees): Candy will create a thin thread or ribbon when dropped from a spoon. (Syrup)

Soft ball (234 degrees): When dropped into water, candy will form into a ball that is moldable when handled. (Fudge)

Firm ball (244 degrees): This ball will hold a good shape but flatten when pressed. (Caramel)

Equivalent Pan Sizes

- Use two 8-inch layer pans or 1 to 2 dozen cupcakes in muffin tins.
- Use three 8-inch layer pans or two 9-inch square pans.
- Use one 9-inch layer pan or one 8-inch square pan.
- Use two 9-inch layer pans or one 9x13 pan or one 9-inch tube pan or two 8-inch square pans.
- Use one 5x9 loaf pan or 2 dozen cupcakes in muffin tins.

A happy home is not one without problems, but one that handles them with understanding and love.

DAVID AND LAURA BYLER,
NEW CASTLE, PA

Measurements Cheat Sheet

½ tablespoon = 1½ teaspoons

1 tablespoon = 3 teaspoons

¼ cup = 4 tablespoons

⅓ cup = 5 tablespoons + 1 teaspoon

½ cup = 8 tablespoons

½ pint = 1 cup (or 8 fluid ounces)

1 pint = 2 cups (or 16 fluid ounces)

1 quart = 4 cups (or 2 pints or 32 ounces)

1 gallon = 16 cups (or 4 quarts)

1 pound = 16 ounces

1 peck = 8 quarts

1 bushel = 4 pecks

Measuring Tips

Some recipes will call for a pinch or a dash of salt or other ingredient. Experienced cooks get a feel for what those mean, but a beginning cook can use this general reference:

Tad = ¼ teaspoon

Dash = ⅛ teaspoon

Pinch = $^1/_{16}$ teaspoon

Smidgen = $^1/_{32}$ teaspoon

A pint of example is worth a barrel full of advice.

CANNING AND PRESERVING

Give her of the fruit
of her hands;
and let her own works
praise her in the gates.

PROVERBS 31:31

CANNING

SLICED APPLES

If you cut up apples the night before making applesauce, do not wash the apples or wet them in any way. Wash them the next day before cooking and they will not turn brown.

EMMA KURTZ, SMICKSBURG, PA

APPLESAUCE COLORING

Add a few vitamin C caplets when cooking apples for applesauce and you'll have nice-looking light yellow apples instead of brown.

RACHEL MILLER, MILLERSBURG, OH

APPLESAUCE FROM PEELINGS

After you have canned your apple pie filling, you have a bunch of peelings and cores left. Don't throw them out. I cook them in water then put them through a strainer. I get a dark applesauce that works perfectly for making apple butter. You will be surprised by how much sauce this makes.

EMMA KURTZ, SMICKSBURG, PA
JOHN LLOYD AND SUSAN YODER, NEWAYGO, MI

PREPPING STRAWBERRIES

It is best to pick strawberries when they are firm and red. However, berries that are a little green will ripen if you leave them on the kitchen counter. Since berries are fragile, use small, shallow containers when picking to avoid crushing. An egg slicer is a quick way to make perfect slices. Also, using a pastry blender for mashing strawberries is quicker than using a fork. A potato masher works well too.

KATHRYN DETWEILER, WEST FARMINGTON, OH

Beets Tip

When you are cooking a large pot of red beets to can, it doesn't need to cook and sputter, making a big mess on your kitchen stove. Instead, cook your pot of beets in the evening on medium heat with a lid on for 10 minutes. Turn off the heat and leave the lid on. Let the beets sit overnight. They will be soft, cooled, and ready to peel and can. Remember to strain some of the beet water to use in your recipes for lovely red coloring.

RUTH M. YODER, BERLIN, PA

Divide the Work

When canning salsa, I like to do most of the chopping of vegetables on one day then do the canning the next morning. Somehow it lessens the stress for me, especially since we sell produce and it is a busy season.

REBECCA HOCHSTETLER, CENTERVILLE, MI

Canning by Water Bath

- When water bath canning, if you have hard water, add ¼ cup vinegar to your water. This will prevent film from building up on jars and the canner.

MIRIAM BYLER, SPARTANSBURG, PA

SADIE BYLER, REYNOLDSVILLE, PA

REBECCA HERSCHBERGER, BEAR LAKE, MI

EMMA KURTZ, SMICKSBURG, PA

MRS. HENRY J. SWARTZENTRUBER, LIBERTY, KY

- When you are water bath canning something like meat with grease that boils out of the jars, add a squirt of dish soap to the canner water. You will be amazed that the grease disappears.

MIRIAM BYLER, SPARTANSBURG, PA

SADIE BYLER, FRAZEYSBURG, OH

- Add vinegar and a bit of dish detergent to the water when processing canned goods, especially meat. The jars will stay cleaner.

MENNO J. YODER FAMILY, BERLIN, PA

Canning Tips

Syrup for Canning Fruit
Heavy syrup: 1 cup sugar to 1 cup water
Medium syrup: 1 cup sugar to 2 cups water
Light syrup: 1 cup sugar to 3 to 4 cups water

- When canning sweet cherries, use light syrup. Too much sugar makes them wrinkle.
- A light syrup of 1 cup sugar and 4 cups water is plenty sweet for peaches.
- Add vitamin C powder to applesauce when canning to retain its yellow color. We add no sugar.

ELIZABETH SHETLER, BRINKHAVEN, OH

Canning Brown Rice

Put ¾ cup dry brown rice in a quart jar and fill with water. Add salt to taste (about ¼ teaspoon per quart). Cold pack for 3 hours. For a pint jar, put in ¼ cup dry rice. This is an inexpensive and easy way to quickly add a side to your meal.

Mrs. Reuben (Anna) Lapp, Rockville, IN

Canning Green Beans

- Green beans have a better flavor if you don't fill the jars with water. Just add enough to dissolve the salt on top.

Emma Kurtz, Smicksburg, PA

- When canning jade beans, put 1 zinc tablet on top of beans in the canning jar. Zinc keeps the beans looking nice and green.

Katie Yoder, Sugarcreek, OH

Canning Corn or Beans

When canning corn or beans, add 1 teaspoon lemon juice to each pint. Makes beans taste like fresh.

Mary Ann Byler, New Wilmington, PA

Canning Peaches

Adding a peach pit or two to each jar of peaches when canning adds flavor and more vibrant color. Put them in the jar first, then add peaches and can as usual.

Mrs. Bethany Martin, Homer City, PA

Meatballs

Make your favorite meatball recipe. Drop mixture with a cookie scoop onto cookie sheet. Bake at 450 degrees until done. Cool. Can be frozen. Or put in jars with barbecue sauce and cold pack for 2½ hours until sealed. Very convenient to have ready meatballs on hand.

Rachel Miller, Millersburg, OH

Granola Storage Tip

When crisping granola in the oven, have canning jars on the stove top to warm. When granola is crisp, put in jars and put lids and rings on. Turn the jars upside down to help seal, or put jars in the oven for 15 to 20 minutes at 200 degrees. If a jar doesn't seal, I use that first. Saves on freezer space and keeps granola fresh. This technique can also be used with graham cracker crumbs.

Esther L. Miller, Fredericktown, OH

FREEZING

FREEZING VEGETABLES

Cut up carrots, celery, and peppers and freeze each in separate containers. Very handy to use in soups or casseroles. No need to precook before freezing.

NORA MILLER, MILLERSBURG, OH

FREEZING POTATOES

Cut small potatoes into cubes with a vegetable chopper. Cook in water until soft. Drain and freeze. Then they'll be ready for quick use.

NORA MILLER, MILLERSBURG, OH

FREEZING ONIONS

- Onions can be chopped and frozen if they start to spoil before you can use them up.

JOHN LLOYD AND SUSAN YODER, NEWAYGO, MI

- Slice onions and freeze in gallon bags. Whenever you need onions, take out what you need and crumble into soups, stews, and other recipes.

NORA MILLER, MILLERSBURG, OH

Frozen Strawberries

Do your strawberries get rubbery after being frozen or in the locker like mine do? Don't throw them out. Thaw them and squeeze out the juice. Heat the juice and stir in sugar and Perma-Flo paste until you reach desired thickness. Add the strawberries and stir until no globs of strawberries remain. Cool and use as fruit filling.

LENA TROYER, REDDING, IA

Strawberry Freezer Jam

2 to 2½ cups strawberries

1 cup dried pineapple bits
or 4 dried rings

Put strawberries and pineapple in blender and blend until smooth. Add water if it is too thick or dry. Makes an easy but delicious jam to eat right away or store in the freezer.

MARY STOLTZFUS, NOTTINGHAM, PA

The recipe doesn't require sugar, but you can add 1 to 2 tablespoons sugar to each batch. Easy, fun, and delicious!

MRS. REUBEN (ANNA) LAPP, ROCKVILLE, IN

Freeze Your Sauces

Wondering what to do with that leftover pasta sauce? Pour it into an ice cube tray, cover, and freeze for later use.

*Happiness is like jam;
you can't spread
even a little without
getting some of
it on yourself.*

Dehydration

Drying Sweet Corn

Cook corn on the cob for 3 minutes. Cut off kernels and spread on flat pans to dry. Dry in oven at 250 degrees, stirring often. When completely dry, store in glass jars.

Salomie E. Glick, Howard, PA

Parsley

To dry your own parsley flakes, cut leaves off the plant and lay them on cookie sheets. Dry in oven with oven door open. When completely dried, crumble with your hands until fine.

Malinda M. Gingerich, Spartansburg, PA

Drying Tea and Parsley

To dry tea or parsley, heat oven to 200 degrees and turn off. Spread tea or parsley on cookie sheet and place in preheated oven. The tea is usually dry by the time the oven cools. If not, heat the oven again for a short time. Drying this way usually keeps the green color.

Mrs. Josep Miller, Navarre, OH

Oven

Want to dehydrate veggies or meats but don't own one of those fancy dehydrators? Use your oven instead. Cut food into ¼-inch slices and place on lined baking sheet. Set your oven on the lowest possible setting for 6 to 8 hours.

Cold Storage

Short-Term Storing Vegetables

- Most fruits and vegetables store best for a few days in the refrigerator wrapped in plastic.
- Asparagus and herbs should be placed upright in water in the refrigerator.
- To keep celery nice for weeks, wrap it in aluminum foil before putting it in the refrigerator.
- Always store your tomatoes and eggplant on the counter.

Garlic

Garlic should be stored in a dry, airy place away from light. Garlic cloves can be kept in the freezer. When ready to use, chop before thawing. Garlic buds will never dry out if stored in a bottle of cooking oil, and when the garlic's gone, you can use oil for salads.

Betty Miller, Goshen, IN

Green Tomatoes

Wrap green tomatoes in newspaper and store in a cool, dark place, and they will ripen nicely.

Mrs. Levi O. Schwartz, Berne, IN

Lemons

Store whole lemons in a closed jar of water in the refrigerator, and when you juice them they will yield more juice.

Betty Miller, Goshen, IN

Storing Potatoes

- Potatoes keep much better over the winter if you wait to dig them until their skins are thick and set. If you dig potatoes and you can rub skin off with your thumb, they are not set yet. Wait awhile longer to dig them up.

    Malinda M. Gingerich, Spartansburg, PA

- Potatoes will keep longer if kept in cool, dry place, stored in a brown paper bag.

    Betty Miller, Goshen, IN

- Dust seed potatoes with lime when you put them in the basement for winter so they keep better and have less rot.

    Mrs. Levi J. Stutzman, West Salem, OH

Root Vegetables

To keep root vegetables over winter in the basement, take plastic 5-gallon buckets—one for each (e.g., beets, carrots, turnips). Fill buckets with vegetables; then lightly cover them with sand. Set in a cool place in the basement. Vegetables will stay nice and crisp. A cover may be set loosely on top if needed.

    Sadie Byler, Frazeysburg, OH

Carrots

In the fall, don't dig your carrots. Put straw bales over them. Through winter, when you need carrots, roll back the bale and dig them up. Roll the bale back over remaining carrots when done.

    Joann Miller, Fredericktown, OH

Doing nothing is hard because you never know when you are done.

David and Laura Byler, New Castle, PA

Storing Beets and Carrots

- Store red beets and carrots in buckets and fill with dry dirt to keep them from getting rubbery.

  Mrs. Joseph Schwartz, Berne, IN

- To keep carrots over winter, put a layer of garden dirt in the bottom of a 5-gallon bucket. Put a layer of unwashed carrots upright on top. Cover with a layer of garden dirt, but don't cover the tops. Store in a dark basement room.

  Katie Petersheim, Lakeview, MI

Storing Pumpkins and Winter Squash

- For long storage life when harvesting winter squash, it is important to leave some of the stem attached to the squash. The best way to ensure this happens is to use a stout knife to separate the stem from the vine. After harvesting, let your squash cure in a warm place (75 to 80 degrees) for 10 days or so. When ready for storage, the outer skin should be very firm. Store winter squash in a cool (around 60 degrees) place that is well ventilated. Humidity should be low at 30 to 50 percent.

  Mrs. Reuben (Anna) Lapp, Rockville, IN

- Lay pumpkins and squash in storage on the same side on which they grew in the garden. The seeds have settled to that side. When the vegetables are placed on the reverse side, the seeds tear away from the sides, causing decay. They say this was practiced by the pioneers.

  Crystal Ropp, Kalona, IA

The dictionary is the only place where success comes before work.

HOUSEHOLD CLEANING TIPS

*For where two or three
are gathered together in my name,
there am I in the midst of them.*

MATTHEW 18:20

Live Deodorizer

A pot of live mint can help neutralize odors in a kitchen, bathroom, nursery, or laundry room.

Homemade Air Fresheners

- To make your own room air freshener, cut an orange in half, remove pulp, and fill peel with salt. This has proven effective in absorbing strong odors all around the house.

  Rebecca Herschberger, Bear Lake, MI

- To remove household odors, put a few drops of wintergreen essential oil (buy at a drugstore) on a cotton ball. Place a ball out of sight in each room.

  Salomie E. Glick, Howard, PA

- Dry orange peels and use in air freshener sachets. Or simmer on stove with cinnamon sticks, whole cloves, lemons, and the like for a delicious smell during winter months.

  Levi and Mary Miller, Junction City, OH

Musty Basement Smell

To get rid of musty basement smells, put charcoal in a flat 1x2-foot box and sprinkle with 1 pint Epsom salt. Scattering a few charcoals here and there also works.

  Mattie Stoltzfus, Paradise, PA

Smoky Room

Burned the toast or forgot to open the vent in the fireplace? A room can be cleared of smoke in a few minutes if you dip a large towel in equal parts vinegar and hot water. Wring it out and wave the towel gently overhead as you walk around the room.

Smell Remover

- To remove smell in milk cans, wastebaskets, iceboxes, and so forth, put vanilla on a cotton ball and leave it inside the container for several hours or days.

  Miriam Byler, Spartansburg, PA

- Salt also deodorizes thermos bottles and jugs.

  Mattie Stoltzfus, Paradise, PA

CLEAN WASTE CANS

To keep your kitchen and other large waste cans clean, put newspaper in the bottom. Then you can easily change the paper as needed.

MIRIAM BYLER, SPARTANSBURG, PA

BATHROOM TRASH

For a sweet-smelling bathroom, place a fabric softener sheet in the wastepaper basket.

MRS. MONROE MILLER, BLANCHARD, MI

BERRY-STAINED HANDS

If you have stains on your hands from picking berries, wash them with a little bottled lemon juice. It will remove the stains in a jiffy.

RUTH BYLER, QUAKER CITY, OH

PAINT ON HANDS

If you have oil-based paint or stain on your hands, try rubbing them with margarine. It removes the paint or stain and leaves your skin soft.

RUTH BYLER, QUAKER CITY, OH

Let everyone sweep in front of his own door and the whole world will be clean.

DAVID AND LAURA BYLER, NEW CASTLE, PA

Uses for Vinegar

- Put vinegar and water in a teakettle that has calcium buildup inside. Let it slowly simmer for a while. It helps dissolve the calcium.
- Add vinegar to a child's potty and let it sit a few hours or overnight. Brush it clean. You should have a nice potty again.

  Levi and Mary Miller, Junction City, OH

- For streak-free windows, put a little vinegar in the water to wash windows.

  Mrs. Henry A. Swartzentruber, Liberty, KY

- Vinegar can be used in a lot of cleaning and in the bathtub for a relaxing bath.
- Mix equal parts vinegar and Dawn dish soap. Heat it a little so it mixes well. Put in a spray bottle. It is good for cleaning stoves, sinks, and more.

  Mrs. Levi J. Stutzman, West Salem, OH

- Mix equal amounts vinegar, liquid soap, and water to clean the bathtub.

  John Lloyd and Susan Yoder, Newaygo, MI

- Boil a cup of vinegar and pour into drain. Or put a handful of baking soda into the drain followed by ½ cup vinegar. Cover drain tightly for a few minutes. Flush with cold water.

  Mrs. Levi J. Stutzman, West Salem, OH

- For washing floors, use some vinegar in your wash water. It keeps the floors shiny. Vinegar is also great for washing windows.

  Miriam Brenneman, Morley, MI

- To stop ants from invading your kitchen, simply wash and spray countertops, cabinets, and floors with equal parts vinegar and water.

  Mary E. Miller, Middlebury, IN

- Mix salt and vinegar and rub on copper-bottom kettles to shine them.

  Mrs. Dan Gingerich, Mount Ayr, IA
  Mrs. Monroe Miller, Blanchard, MI

Uses for Baking Soda

- Baking soda or washing soda can be used for many things around the home. If vinegar alone doesn't do the job, sometimes adding baking soda helps. I use soda instead of Comet for many cleaning jobs. Soda is not as abrasive.

  Mrs. Levi J. Stutzman, West Salem, OH

- Put baking soda in dishwater to make the dishes shine.

  Verna Gingerich, Mount Ayr, IA

China Stains

Baking powder will remove tea and coffee stains from china pots and cups.

Ruth Byler, Quaker City, OH

No-Streak Windows

- For clean, streak-free windows, wash with a wet microfiber cloth and dry with a flour sack towel.

  Susan Schwartz, Berne, IN

- For streak-free windows and mirrors, wipe the cleaner off with newspaper instead of paper towels.

  Crystal Ropp, Kalona, IA

Winter Window Spray

Put rubbing alcohol and vinegar in warm water to clean windows in winter so they won't frost in the process.

Rachel Miller, Millersburg, OH
Mrs. Dan Gingerich, Mount Ayr, IA

Ammonia for Glass

Add a small amount of ammonia to washing water to make glassware sparkle. Ammonia is also good for washing windows. Polish windows with crumpled newspaper.

ERG, Salem, IN

Crystal-Clear Glass Containers

Do your flower vases or coffee carafes have stains or water rings that are hard to clean? Put one or two denture cleanser tablets into the vase or carafe and fill with warm water. The fizzing action dissolves stains in minutes. Rinse with clean water, and if there is still a stubborn spot, repeat the process.

Malinda M. Gingerich, Spartansburg, PA

If it wouldn't be for the last minute, some of us wouldn't get anything done.

David and Laura Byler, New Castle, PA

CLEANING SMALL BOTTLES

To clean small glass bottles, put in 1 or 2 teaspoons of vinegar, then add a few grains of dry rice. Shake well, then rinse.

CLEANING A TEAKETTLE

- To clean a teakettle on the inside, try using tomato juice. Even old and moldy juice will work. Add an equal amount of water to the juice. Fill the kettle and let it sit overnight. Wash in the morning.

  MRS. LEVI J. STUTZMAN, WEST SALEM, OH

- To clean a teakettle, use ¼ cup vinegar and 3 teaspoons salt. Boil for 15 minutes. Saves a lot of scrubbing.

  RUTH BYLER, QUAKER CITY, OH

STAINLESS STEEL

To clean stainless steel without streaks, use Windex and dry it. It works better than stainless steel polish.

MARY ANN BYLER, NEW WILMINGTON, PA

STAINED STAINLESS STEEL

To clean stains from stainless steel cookware, put some lemon juice in the pan and wipe it out. No rubbing or scrubbing is necessary. The pan will be shiny once again.

RUTH BYLER, QUAKER CITY, OH

COPPER CLEANER

Instead of buying special cleaner for your copper kettles, try Worcestershire sauce for polishing. It doesn't take much and really does the job.

RUTH BYLER, QUAKER CITY, OH

CLEANING PANS

To clean cookie sheets, cupcake pans, and roast pans, spray with oven cleaner. Let sit awhile. When washed they come out sparkling clean.

ANNA KING, NEW CASTLE, IN

STUBBORN TARNISH

To remove tarnish from silver, find a cook pan larger than the silver piece and place a piece of aluminum foil or an empty aluminum can in the pan with the tarnished silver. In 1 quart warm water, dissolve 1 teaspoon salt and 1 teaspoon baking soda. Pour over aluminum and bring water to a boil. Boil gently until the tarnish is removed. Dry and polish the silver to a satiny shine.

Stove

To clean your stove without leaving streaks, use a clean, wet rag. To remove grease splatters, wash with a soapy cloth before grease hardens.

Miriam Byler, Spartansburg, PA

Slick Stove

To help keep your cookstove clean, scrub the top and spray with silicone spray. Dirt will slide off instead of burning onto it.

Menno J. Yoder family, Berlin, PA

Oven Cleaner

- Dissolve 2 heaping tablespoons lye in ½ cup cold water in a glass jar. In another container, stir 1 level tablespoon cornstarch in ½ cup cold water. Pour cornstarch solution slowly into warm lye, stirring constantly. Apply to the inside of oven. Let sit awhile then wipe off.

Emma Byler, New Wilmington, PA

- When needing to clean the oven, put a glass container of ammonia inside the oven the night before to make for ease of cleaning the next day.

Rebecca Hochstetler, Centerville, MI

- After a spill in the oven, soak a cloth in ammonia and leave it on the burnt spill area for an hour or so. You will then be able to scrape off the spot easily without harming the enamel.

Ruth Byler, Quaker City, OH

Stove Parts

In the evening, put grates or stove parts that need major cleaning in a large garbage bag and pour 2 cups ammonia into bag and close tightly. Let sit until morning. Parts will be easy to wash. Do not inhale ammonia!

Kate Bontrager, Middlebury, IN

Stove Top Preserver

I use original Armor All to keep the stove top smooth. It cleans easier and prevents rust. Spray some on and wipe down with a towel. I've heard some use furniture polish now, but I haven't tried it yet. I also put Armor All in the oven, and spills wipe up easier.

Levi and Mary Miller, Junction City, OH

Chimney Tip

Put an aluminum pop can in your woodstove every week to keep your chimney clean.

Edith N. Christner, Berne, IN

Weekly Drain Treatment

- Maintain free-flowing pipes with this weekly treatment. Combine ¼ cup baking soda, ¼ cup salt, and 1 tablespoon cream of tartar and stir thoroughly. Pour mixture down the drain; then immediately follow with a cup of boiling water. Wait a few seconds; then rinse with cold water.

  DAVID AND LAURA BYLER, NEW CASTLE, PA

- To keep the sink drainpipe clean, put 1 or 2 tablespoons lye in the pipe followed by pouring some hot water in.

  MRS. HENRY A. SWARTZENTRUBER, LIBERTY, KY

Clogged Drain

- Unclog your drain with white vinegar. Pour ½ cup baking soda down the drain followed by a cup of hot vinegar. Let the two bubble and break apart the debris. After a few minutes, flush the drain with a quart of hot water. It's natural, safe, and won't damage pipes.

  DAVID AND LAURA BYLER, NEW CASTLE, PA

- Mix ½ cup baking soda and ½ cup salt together. Pour into the drain. Follow with 1 jug of vinegar. You will see foam and bubbles rise out of the drain. Let it sit for 10 to 20 minutes. Turn on the hot water and let run for 20 to 30 seconds; then run the same amount of cold water. The drain should now run freely.

  RUTH BYLER, QUAKER CITY, OH

- For clogged drains, pour ¼ cup lye into drain followed by 1 cup hot water.

  MIRIAM BYLER, SPARTANSBURG, PA

- To remove grease buildup in drains, dump ½ cup salt and ½ cup baking soda down the drain. Then pour in a kettleful of boiling water. Allow to sit overnight before rinsing.

  DAVID AND LAURA BYLER, NEW CASTLE, PA

Dish Cloths

To keep dishwashing cloths from getting stinky, wash them out with clean, cold water every time you get done washing dishes.

MRS. JOSEPH SCHWARTZ, BERNE, IN

Mop Tip

Sew an extra Miracle cloth over a wall mop and it will extend the life of the mop.

VERNA GINGERICH, MOUNT AYR, IA

Cleaning with Brushes

Paintbrushes are handy for dusting louvered doors, lampshades, and baseboards. Toothbrushes are great for cleaning hard-to-reach places such as tile grout, faucets, knobs, shirt cuffs and collars, graters, colanders, and so on.

Cleaning Hairbrushes

To clean hairbrushes, use a wide-tooth comb or pick to remove hair. Fill sink with warm water and a generous splash of ammonia or shampoo. Swish brush around for a minute. All plastic brushes and combs can be soaked for several minutes. For stubborn spots, use an old toothbrush to remove dirt. Rinse and dry in a well-ventilated area.

To Clean a Broom

Add some dish soap and a generous amount of salt to lukewarm water. Dunk and swish the broom (or brush) several times. Rinse and dry outside in the sun.

A good temperature is a cool head and a warm heart.

The best place to
find a helping
hand is at the end
of your arm.

Mark Remover

Use lemon oil to take permanent marker, crayon, or scuff marks off floors, walls, and so forth.

MARY ELLEN MILLER, APPLE CREEK, OH
RACHEL KUEFER, KINCARDINE, ONTARIO, CANADA

Sticky Residue

To remove sticky adhesive, rub with olive oil, butter, peanut butter, baby oil, or the like and wipe clean.

MIRIAM BYLER, SPARTANSBURG, PA

Paint Remover

To remove paint or varnish, use 2 parts ammonia and 1 part turpentine.

MALINDA M. GINGERICH, SPARTANSBURG, PA

Rug Brushing

When brushing a carpet or large rug, first dip the brush or broom in cold, salted water and shake off the excess. This will keep down the dust and freshen the carpet.

Carpet/Rug Stains

- For grease or ink spots on carpet, immediately cover with salt. Scoop up the salt as it absorbs the stain and repeat until the salt comes up clean. Put on more and leave overnight to be sure all is absorbed.
- Candle wax spilled on carpet can be removed by letting it dry and harden then covering with a lightweight cloth. Press the cloth with a warm iron to melt the wax, and let it absorb into the cloth. Keep moving the cloth to a clean patch for fresh absorption and to keep from sending absorbed wax back into your rug.

Trash Tip

- Put a roll of trash bags in the bottom of a wastebasket. It is always there when you take the full bag out and need another one.

ESTHER L. MILLER, FREDERICKTOWN, OH

- A handful of dry laundry detergent scattered in the bottom of garbage cans will help repel flies and other insects.

A Clean Buggy

Spray Armor All tire shine on buggy to making cleaning easier.

MRS. DAN GINGERICH, MOUNT AYR, IA

Recipes for
HOMEMADE CLEANING PRODUCTS

BEST SIMPLE CLEANER

1 cup ammonia
½ cup vinegar

¼ cup baking soda
1 gallon water

Mix all ingredients together and use for cleaning anything. It's great on walls.

EDITH N. CHRISTNER, BERNE, IN

AMAZING CLEANER

1 cup lye
2 cups Gain or other liquid soap

½ cup ammonia
2½ gallons water

Mix all ingredients and use to wash walls. Mixture will take dirt off about anything. Put in a spray bottle and spray on lunch boxes and other things; then wash off and watch the dirt roll away.

EMMA BYLER, NEW WILMINGTON, PA

ALL-PURPOSE CLEANER

1 tablespoon Sisel
  laundry detergent
1 tablespoon Sisel OrganiCleanse

3 cups white vinegar
1 teaspoon baking soda
1 teaspoon lemon essential oil

Mix all ingredients and use on floors, furniture, appliances, and even windows.

MRS. REUBEN N. BYLER, DAYTON, PA

Homemade Mean Green Cleaner

1 cup laundry detergent
1 cup bleach
½ cup lye
3 gallons hot water

Mix all together and use for tough cleaning jobs.

Lizzie Christner, Berne, IN

House Cleaner

2 cups water
15 drops essential lemon
or lavender oil
15 drops essential rosemary oil
15 drops tea tree oil

In a spray bottle, mix water with essential oils. Shake bottle before each use.

Ruthie Miller, Loudonville, OH

Citrus Cleaner

Save lemon, orange, or grapefruit peels. Fill a jar ⅔ full of citrus peels, fill with vinegar, and let sit for 2 to 4 weeks. Strain out the peels and put liquid in a spray bottle. Add lemon or tea tree oil for added strength. Makes a good cleaner.

Lydia Ruth Byler, Newburg, PA

Homemade Mild Sink Soap

Mix together ½ cup Dawn dish soap and 2 cups vinegar in spray bottle. Shake well before each use. We like this better than the brand-name versions. This is not as harsh and works great.

Susan Bontrager, Lagrange, IN

The secret to success is to start from scratch and then keep on scratching.

Gentle Cleanser

Do you get dry, cracked hands from housecleaning? Try using a teaspoon of baking soda in a gallon of warm water with a few drops of lemon or lavender oil to clean with using a Miracle cloth.

Mrs. Reuben N. Byler, Dayton, PA

Liquid All-Purpose Cleaning Soap

2½ gallons rainwater
1¾ cups lye
1 cup ammonia
2 cups liquid detergent (I like Gain)
1 cup powdered detergent (I like Gain)

Fill 5-gallon pail half full of cold rainwater. Add lye, ammonia, liquid detergent, and powdered detergent. Stir to dissolve, about 15 minutes. Let sit 30 minutes, then stir well. Fill bucket with water and stir thoroughly. Leave in bucket with lid or store in bottles. Keep stirring soap as you dip it out, as it will settle. Always stir or shake before using. Can be used for laundry, walls, ceiling, floors, furniture, and so on.

Amanda Byler, Curwensville, PA

She who chooses a job she likes will never have to work a day in her life.

Natural Bleach

12 cups water
1 cup peroxide
¼ cup lemon juice

Combine all ingredients and store in vinegar jug. Keep tightly closed. Spray on stains and let sit 10 minutes before washing. It may discolor colored clothing. Also useful for cleaning countertops. Cleaning power will decline after a month.

RACHEL D. MILLER, MILLERSBURG, OH

Bleach Alternative

1½ cups 3 percent hydrogen peroxide
½ cup lemon juice
Water to fill 1-gallon jar

Mix ingredients and store in glass jar. Use 1 cup solution per load of laundry.

MARY ELLEN STOLTZFUS, GAP, PA

Shower Cleaner

⅓ cup Dawn dishwashing soap
12 ounces white vinegar
Water

Combine soap and vinegar in quart-sized spray bottle. Fill bottle with water. Use to clean showers and sinks. Works great to cut soap scum.

RUTH HOCHSTETLER, DUNDEE, OH

Mildew Remover

2 quarts water
½ cup vinegar
½ cup bleach

Combine ingredients. Soak mildew spots several hours or overnight. Rinse and dry.

ANNA ZOOK, DALTON, OH

Simple Window Cleaner

Put 1 tablespoon Dawn dish soap and ¼ cup rubbing alcohol in a spray bottle. Fill with water.

Mrs. Christine Schmidt, Salem, IN

Window Spray

1 pint rubbing alcohol
1 pint vinegar
1 teaspoon dish soap
½ cup ammonia (optional)

In a clean plastic jug that has a lid, add alcohol, vinegar, and dish soap. Fill three-fourths full with water and mix. Clearly mark jug as "window spray" and store in a cool place. To label the jug, I use a marker to draw a picture of a window with curtains on so that it is easier to spot among other such jugs. Keep out of reach of children.

S.H., PA

Lemon Window Cleaner

1 cup vinegar
10 to 15 drops lemon essential oil
Distilled water

Put vinegar and lemon oil in 1-quart container and fill with distilled water.

Regina Bontrager, Lagrange, IN

Window Cleaner

Use equal parts rubbing alcohol and water with a drop of bluing in a spray bottle.

Salomie E. Glick, Howard, PA

Homemade Windex

1 pint rubbing alcohol
3 tablespoons liquid detergent
2 tablespoons ammonia
3 drops blue food coloring

Put ingredients in a gallon jug and add water to fill the gallon. Put in a spray bottle to use on windows.

Schwartz family, Salem, IN
Miriam Brenneman, Morley, MI
Lizzie Christner, Berne, IN
Mrs. Monroe Miller, Blanchard, MI

May the hinges of friendship never grow rusty.

Cookware Cleaner

1 cup lye	1 cup laundry detergent
1 cup bleach	

Fill a stainless steel canner three-fourths full of warm water. Add lye, bleach, and laundry detergent. Heat to almost boiling. Remove handles and knobs from your stainless steel cookware. Wearing rubber gloves, dip all your stainless steel cookware and silverware in the solution. It will come out nice and shiny. Use only on stainless steel.

Mrs. Josep Miller, Navarre, OH

Furniture Cleaner

Use lemon oil to clean furniture. Put a few drops of lemon oil in water. Gives a refreshing smell.

John Lloyd and Susan Yoder, Newaygo, MI

Furniture Polish

12 ounces warm water	1 teaspoon Borax
2 tablespoons vinegar	A few drops tea tree oil

Combine all ingredients and put in a spray bottle.

Mrs. Reuben N. Byler, Dayton, PA

Citrus Dusting Spray

2 teaspoons olive oil	¼ cup vinegar
1 teaspoon lemon or orange oil	1 cup water

Combine all ingredients in a spray bottle. Spray on a piece of cheesecloth, and then wipe wooden furniture. A little goes a long way. Mix well before each use.

Ada J. Mast, Kalona, IA

Unless you put out your water jars when it rains, you won't catch any water.

PEST DETERRENTS

PEPPERMINT OIL

- Add a few drops of peppermint oil to water when cleaning floors and wood-work. Helps keep flies and spiders away.

  ESTHER L. MILLER, FREDERICKTOWN, OH

- Drop peppermint oil beside places where you think mice might enter the house. Mice detest the smell of peppermint.

  MALINDA M. GINGERICH, SPARTANSBURG, PA

OSAGE ORANGES

Osage oranges (or hedge apples) are good to put around in places where spiders and insects are. I keep them in the storerooms. One or two might be used in the canning room.

S.H., PA

ALL-NATURAL INSECT REPELLENT

1 cup witch hazel
1 cup distilled water or
  aloe vera juice
15 drops lemongrass essential oil
10 drops eucalyptus essential oil

10 drops citronella essential oil
10 drops tea tree essential oil
5 drops lavender essential oil
5 drops cedarwood essential oil

Mix all ingredients in spray bottle. Shake well before each use. Apply to body every 2 to 3 hours to repel insects. Note: Avoid eye contact and broken skin.

SARAH ESH, KINZERS, PA

Spider Deterrent

Spiders don't like to walk where lemon furniture polish or lemon essential oil has recently been sprayed.

David and Laura Byler, New Castle, PA

Fly and Spider Deterrent

1 gallon water	5 drops lemon essential oil
10 drops peppermint essential oil	10 drops Dawn dish detergent

Combine ingredients and spray your porches and around the inside of your house. Can also be used to mop your floors. Spiders don't like the smell and stay away.

Sadie Byler, Reynoldsville, PA

Fly Spray

3 cups water	1 cup Avon Skin So Soft bath oil
2 cups white vinegar	1 tablespoon eucalyptus oil

Put all ingredients in jar and shake. Use as wipe or spray. Lasts 2 to 3 days and keeps flies and mosquitoes away!

Esta Miller, Millersburg, OH

Easy Fly Trap

Fill a plastic jar three-fourths full with water. Add ¼ cup apple cider vinegar, 2 tablespoons sugar, and 2 tablespoons dish soap. Use a very strong string and put the ends down in the jar, leaving it long enough to hang. Screw on the lid over the string. Punch a few holes in the lid so flies can get in. Hang jar on porch or other places around the yard. Works amazingly well.

Esther Miller, Rossiter, PA

Control your attitude, or it will control you.

Pantry Bugs

To keep bugs out of flour and other grains, tape a bay leaf inside the bag or canister lid but not touching the flour.

Ant Repellent

- A few crumbled bay leaves will discourage ants from invading your cupboards.
  SADIE BYLER, REYNOLDSVILLE, PA

- A good way to keep ants out of the house in summer is to keep powered sulfur around the house. We like to sprinkle it around the house once a week. Twice a week is even better.
  MRS. HENRY A. SWARTZENTRUBER, LIBERTY, KY

- Mix equal parts Borax and white sugar. Scatter around the outside of your house or wherever you have problems with ants.
  EMMA BYLER, NEW WILMINGTON, PA

- Ants do not like peppermint. You can use peppermint tea leaves or essential oil wherever you see a path of ants.
  DAVID AND LAURA BYLER, NEW CASTLE, PA

Gnat and Fruit Fly Trap

Put 1 tablespoon honey and 1 teaspoon dishwashing liquid in either a cup of warm water or a cup of apple cider vinegar. This bait mixture draws gnats and fruit flies and often drowns them. I put the mixture in a plastic gallon milk jug and poke holes in it so the insects can get in but not out. If you see a few stragglers escaping, sit by the jug with a spray bottle of rubbing alcohol and spray the gnats as they appear. Do this daily until they vanish for good.
DAVID AND LAURA BYLER, NEW CASTLE, PA
MALINDA M. GINGERICH, SPARTANSBURG, PA

Wasp Deterrent

Keep mothballs outdoors in places where you don't want wasps to build nests.
REBECCA HERSCHBERGER, BEAR LAKE, MI

Tick Deterrent

To keep ticks off your body, eat black walnuts and take black walnut tincture. Ticks hate walnuts, so they will dislike that taste in the blood.
AARON AND EMMA GINGERICH, BREMEN, OH

Bug Band

Tie a piece of baler twine (not plastic) around your neck and around your wrist or ankle. It will keep bugs away.
KATIE W. YODER, GOSHEN, IN

If you think you know everything,
you have a lot to learn.

LAUNDRY

Now ye are clean through the word
which I have spoken unto you.

JOHN 15:3

LAUNDRY SOAP

Fill five 1-gallon pails half full of water (rainwater works best)
Add:

12 ounces lye	2 cups Borax
7 cups grease, melted (½ tallow and ½ lard works well)	3 cups Wisk or any desired detergent
1 cup ammonia	

Mix lye, grease, ammonia, Borax, and detergent. Divide evenly into five 1-gallon pails of water and stir well. Finish filling the gallon pails with water. Several times a day, stir for a few minutes. Do this for 6 or 7 days. Then cover and store until ready to use.

MRS. CHRIS HOSTETLER, NORWALK, WI

HOMEMADE LAUNDRY SOAP

1 bar Fels Naptha soap	2 cups Arm & Hammer washing soda powder
1 gallon boiling water	2½ cups Seventh Generation liquid laundry soap
1½ cups Borax powder	

Shave bar soap into boiling water and stir until melted. Put all ingredients in a 5-gallon bucket and mix well. Fill with water.

RACHEL MILLER, MILLERSBURG, OH

Troubled waters cleanse the garments best.

Homemade Fabric Softener

1 cup hair conditioner	3 cups white vinegar
6 cups hot water	10 drops essential oil

Mix conditioner and hot water well until incorporated. Add vinegar and essential oil. Mix well. Use ¼ cup per load of laundry.

NORA MILLER, MILLERSBURG, OH

Vinegar Fabric Softener

- To 1 gallon vinegar, add 20 drops lavender essential oil for an instant fabric softener. Shake well before each use.

  MRS. REUBEN N. BYLER, DAYTON, PA
- Use 1 cup vinegar and ½ cup baking soda in laundry rinse water for softer laundry.

  MRS. LEVI J. STUTZMAN, WEST SALEM, OH
- A good fabric softener for laundry is 1 or 2 cups vinegar in the rinse water, especially if there's a good breeze blowing. The clothes smell so fresh and clean.

  MRS. HENRY A. SWARTZENTRUBER, LIBERTY, KY

Laundry Presoak Spray

1 cup water	1 cup ammonia
1 cup liquid Wisk	

Pour all ingredients into spray bottle. Spray liberally on soiled areas of clothing. Let saturate, then scrub and toss into washer. This even works for bacon grease and the like.

MARY MILLER, SHIPSHEWANA, IN

Laundry Stain Remover

1 cup Dawn dish detergent	1 cup water
1 cup white vinegar	

Mix together and squirt on stained clothing. Rub a little before laundering.

SADIE BYLER, REYNOLDSVILLE, PA
EMMA BYLER, NEW WILMINGTON, PA

Laundry Stains

- Some stains can be removed from clothes by sponging with full-strength vinegar within 24 hours. Wash out immediately.

  Mrs. Levi J. Stutzman, West Salem, OH

- Drizzle some rubbing alcohol on ink stains. Let sit a couple minutes then wash as usual.

  Mrs. Daniel Wickey, Berne, IN

- For stains on clothes, rub in Murphy's oil soap then wash it out.

  Edith N. Christner, Berne, IN

- Shampoo for oily hair will often remove grease marks on fabric.

- To remove bloodstains, use your own saliva or icy-cold water.

Perspiration Odor

For fresh perspiration on clothes, soak in water with baking soda. For old perspiration, soak in a solution of milk and vinegar.

Wax in Fabric

If your wax candles melt onto the tablecloth, invert and stretch the affected fabric over a bowl and pour boiling water onto it until the wax melts and drips away.

Malinda's Guide for Laundry Stain Removal

Grass: vinegar	**Coffee:** baking soda
Grease: baking soda	**Sweat:** lemon juice
Blood or rust: hydrogen peroxide	**Ink:** rubbing alcohol
Oil: white chalk	

Malinda M. Gingerich, Spartansburg, PA

Paint Spots

Paint spots on clothing will come out with several applications of equal parts ammonia and turpentine.

Lacy Glick, Mill Hall, PA

Gum in Fabric

To remove chewing gum from fabric, rub the gum with an ice cube and it will roll off.

Color Fast

Adding Epsom salt to your laundry water when washing colored garments prevents fading.

MALINDA M. GINGERICH, SPARTANSBURG, PA

Whites

To whiten whites like capes and aprons, mix ½ cup bleach and ½ cup baking soda to a gallon of water and soak the laundry before washing.

LIZZIE CHRISTNER, BERNE, IN

Lint Repellent

To keep lint from clinging to clothes in the wash, put ½ to 1 cup white vinegar in the rinse water.

Lint Catcher

Keep a sieve/strainer in your laundry area to capture lint if your wash or rinse water gets "fuzzy."

MIRIAM BYLER, SPARTANSBURG, PA

It isn't hard to make a mountain out of a molehill; just add a little dirt.

Laundry Delicates

Wring out your bras, onesies, and other delicates by hand instead of putting them through the wringer so hooks, snaps, and the like don't get ruined.

MIRIAM BYLER, SPARTANSBURG, PA

Velcro

Always close Velcro (hook and loop) when you put it in the laundry so it doesn't fray delicate material.

MIRIAM BYLER, SPARTANSBURG, PA

Nylons

Rinse nylon socks and stockings in vinegar water to improve elasticity and prevent runs.

Washing Thick Coats

When washing thick winter coats, put them through the wringer twice after they are rinsed. They dry a lot faster that way.

LEVI AND MARY MILLER, JUNCTION CITY, OH

Curtains

To wash white curtains and not have to iron, add 1 cup Clorox bleach, 1 cup Downy fabric softener, and 1 cup bluing to a machine of cold water. Start the agitator before adding curtains. It is important to use cold water. Immediately hang on the line when done washing.

SADIE BYLER, REYNOLDSVILLE, PA

Solution for Washing Women's Head Coverings

1 ounce liquid Clorox 2	1 ounce liquid Wisk or
1 ounce liquid Cascade detergent	some kind of bluing

Place soaps in 1½-gallon pail and add water. Put as many as three coverings in water and soak for a few hours. Rinse with clear water.

MARILYN HOSTETLER, TOPEKA, IN

Clothes Basket Moving

When hanging out clothes, put the basket of clean clothes in the children's wagon. It will be easy to move along the line, especially if a child is willing to pull it. Keeps the basket clean and keeps you from having to lean down as far. A small wheelbarrow will also work.

Clothes Drying Ring

Remove the rubber tire from a bicycle wheel. Put a rod through the center of the wheel to hang it up by. Drill holes along the rim of the wheel. Space holes however you prefer. Fasten a plastic clothespin with a zip tie through each hole. This creates a very helpful dryer for laundry days. I use it in winter too. Hang it outside for clothes to dry; then bring the ring inside to remove the laundry. I hang one low in the washhouse so a six-year-old can hang up the hankies and more.

Levi and Mary Miller, Junction City, OH

Clotheslines

Use a clothesline on laundry day. There is nothing quite like the smell of clothes dried in the out-of-doors. Also, the sun has a way of taking care of bacteria that the washer and dryer can't.

Freezing Clotheslines

In winter wipe clotheslines with a rag soaked in vinegar. Clothes won't freeze to the line and will be easier to remove.

Mrs. Dan Gingerich, Mount Ayr, IA

Warm Clothespins

Got the blues about hanging out the laundry on cold days? Leave the clothespins in the washhouse where it is warm. Take out just enough to hang up that load. Warm clothespins keep your fingers from getting so cold.

Lovina D. Gingerich, Mount Ayr, IA

A smile adds a great deal to face value.

Home Health Remedies

Let them not depart from thine eyes; keep them in the midst of thine heart. For they are life unto those that find them, and health to all their flesh. Keep thy heart with all diligence; for out of it are the issues of life.

PROVERBS 4:21–23

IMMUNE SUPPORT

PLEASE NOTE: Don't take anything you read here as replacement for your doctor's advice or emergency medical attention. All home remedies should only be used with a healthy dose of common sense and caution.

LAUGH MORE

A hearty laugh gives a workout to your stomach and chest muscles, heart, and lungs. Though your blood pressure and adrenaline go up during laughter, they drop down to normal or below afterward, releasing stress.

MRS. JOSEPH J. SCHWARTZ, SALEM, IN

SIMPLE UNIVERSAL REMEDY

I've found a little remedy to ease the life we live that costs the least and does the most. It is the word *forgive*.

MRS. DAVID KURTZ, SMICKSBURG, PA

GET SOME SUNSHINE

Don't hide from the sun. Daily time spent outdoors in direct and indirect sunlight is good for the body and overall health.

Onion Germ Trap

- I always have a dish of chopped onions sitting out in the living room and kitchen during winter. If some sickness is going around, I put out more dishes. Seems to help.

  Ruth Miller, Millersburg, OH
  Cevilla Swartzentruber, Franklinville, NY

- Cut onions in half and place one in each room of the house. Onions absorb germs and help keep colds and flu away. Change onions as often as necessary. Throw used onions in the trash. A very old and tried remedy.

  Levi and Mary Miller, Junction City, OH

Allergies

Allergies may be helped by consuming locally collected honey in several spoonfuls a day.

Molly Kinsinger, Meyersdale, PA

English Ivy

A tea made from dried English ivy leaves is said to help with cough and allergies, so keep a houseplant of ivy around.

David and Laura Byler, New Castle, PA

Mint Uses

Add mint to your garden. Mint has many uses. Chew a sprig or two for fresh-smelling breath. Use leaves to make a tea to ease stomach pain, nausea, vomiting, and gas. Very soothing for whatever ails you.

Leah Yoder, Glenville, PA

The First Steps to Good Health

Have a smile for everyone,
great and small, rich or poor.
Use respect.
Love thy neighbor as thyself.

Always try to be happy and content
with what you have.

Ruth Byler, Quaker City, OH

Honey Fermented Garlic

Peel 3 bulbs garlic of garlic and lightly crush them (don't completely smash them). Put into a pint jar and add 1 cup raw honey. Be sure to completely cover the garlic and to leave a good inch of headspace at the top of the jar. Tilt or stir the jar to remove air bubbles. Place the lid on and allow the jar to sit on the counter about 4 weeks.

In the beginning, your garlic will want to float to the top. To ensure that it stays covered, stir it every day or flip the jar upside down on day 2, then right side up on day 3, and so forth. In a few days, you should see signs of fermentation (bubbles). If you don't see bubbles after a few days, you may not have enough moisture. Simply add 1 teaspoon water.

For the first 2 weeks, loosen the lid daily to release the fermenting gases. This is called "burping."

As the fermentation slows down, you can burp every few days. Over time the garlic will darken in color, the honey will get runnier, and you will stop seeing bubbles. This is all normal.

Store in a cool, dry, and dark cabinet. Use after 2 to 3 months. No refrigeration is needed. Use the honey garlic in recipes as you wish. I give my children a teaspoonful every day as an immunity booster.

NATHAN AND ANNA FISHER, SALISBURY, PA

Cold Prevention

If starting to get a cold, take some pure olive oil to flush out toxins.

MRS. DAN GINGERICH, MOUNT AYR, IA

The Lord often digs wells of joy with the spade of sorrow.

HEALTH TEAS AND TONICS

ADRENAL COCKTAIL

1 to 2 organic lemons, peeled
1½ cups filtered water
1 teaspoon MCT oil
1 teaspoon protein powder
½ teaspoon vanilla
2 pinches salt
½ teaspoon cinnamon
½ teaspoon turmeric
¼ teaspoon ginger
¼ teaspoon nutmeg
Pinch ground clove
¼ teaspoon stevia
2,000 to 4000 mg
    vitamin C powder
1 to 2 drops lemon Young
    Living essential oil
Ice cubes

Peel lemons, leaving as much white pith as possible for nutritional benefit. (If lemons are organic, you can use the rinds.) Slice lemons in quarters and remove seeds. Place lemons in blender. Add all remaining ingredients besides ice. Blend well. Pour mixture into quart jar and fill to top with ice. Put lid on jar and shake before drinking.

KATIE MILLER, ARTHUR, IL

ARTERY CLEANSE

1 quart apple juice
1 quart cranberry-grape juice
1 cup raw apple cider vinegar

Combine all ingredients. Drink ½ cup on empty stomach every morning.

RUTH HOCHSTETLER, DUNDEE, OH

Arthritis Drink

12 ounces rhubarb concentrate	1 pack yeast
6 cups sugar	

Put ingredients in a gallon jug and fill with water. Let stand 21 days before drinking. Said to cure arthritis.

Mrs. Dan Gingerich, Mount Ayr, IA

Fruit Tonic for Arthritis

6 lemons	6 grapefruit
6 oranges	¼ cup Epsom salt

Grind up fruit peelings and all. Put in a crock. Sprinkle Epsom salt over the mixture. Pour 1 quart boiling water over top. Cover and let stand overnight. Put in a cloth bag and squeeze out the juice. Take 1 tablespoon 3 times a day. Use for at least 2 months.

Emma Byler, New Wilmington, PA

Brain Boost

Rosemary is said to protect your brain and give it a boost. Add 1 teaspoon rosemary leaf to a cup of hot water for health benefits.

David and Laura Byler, New Castle, PA

Booster

Drink a glass of warm water with 1 teaspoon honey and 1 teaspoon apple cider vinegar each day. It does wonders to restore energy and drives away fatigue.

Malinda M. Gingerich, Spartansburg, PA

Echinacea Tonic

2 parts fresh echinacea herb, chopped	1 part peppermint leaves, chopped
1 part fresh echinacea root, chopped	Vodka
	Glycerin

Pack herbs in jar. Mix half vodka and half glycerin to cover herbs. Let stand at room temperature for 4 weeks, shaking daily. Strain and bottle. Use for children and adults as an immune booster.

Mrs. Jonas Gingerich, Dalton, OH

The Great Physician always
has the right remedy.

Elderberry Juice

Gather ripe elderberries. Wash and remove most stems. Put in kettle and cover with equal quantity of water. Bring to boil and simmer 5 minutes. Strain. Pour into jars and process in boiling water bath for 10 minutes. Add honey to serve as a good winter drink. When a child is sick, I put this in a bottle for them to slowly sip. Does wonders.

CEVILLA SWARTZENTRUBER, FRANKLINVILLE, NY

Elderberry Fire Water

½ cup boiling water
1 teaspoon salt
½ to 1 teaspoon cayenne

¼ cup vinegar
¼ cup homemade elderberry
   syrup or Sambucol

Combine all ingredients. Take by teaspoon to ward off colds.

FREIDA FISHER, SPRAKERS, NY

Eldermint Cough Syrup

2 cups fresh elderberry blossoms
2 cups fresh peppermint leaves
2 cups glycerin

2 cups distilled water
   or boiled water

Put all ingredients in glass jar and let sit for 4 to 6 weeks. Shake daily. Strain and bottle. Take 1 tablespoon for cough.

WILLIAM AND REBECCA TROYER, NAVARRE, OH

*In youth we learn;
in age we understand.*

Fire Water

¾ to 1 teaspoon cayenne pepper
1 teaspoon salt
½ cup boiling water
½ cup apple cider vinegar

At the first sign of a sniffle or cold, combine all ingredients and take 1 tablespoon every 15 minutes for 1 hour. Then cut back to 1 tablespoon an hour until entire cup has been consumed.

Linda Miller, Spartansburg, PA
Martha Miller, Decatur, IN
Rebecca E. Stutzman, Gilman, WI

Tried-and-True Good Health Tea

- I often make a cup of tea in the morning with 3 teaspoons apple cider vinegar with mother and 1 teaspoon honey in a cup of hot water. I feel this keeps me from getting sick as often with colds and the like.

  Iva Yoder, Goshen, IN

- Add 1 teaspoon honey and 1 teaspoon apple cider vinegar to a cup of hot tea with lemon. Drink first thing in the morning. Good for sickness prevention, stomach problems, the liver, colitis, and more. May help to get rid of excessive fluid.

  Emma Byler, New Wilmington, PA
  Mary Miller, Junction City, OH
  Lizzie H. Stutzman, Gilman, WI
  Mrs. Christine Schmidt, Salem, IN

- Mix 1 tablespoon apple cider vinegar and 1 tablespoon honey in glass of water. Take upon rising in the morning and before every meal. This drink is good for aches and pains and many other things.

  Emma A. Hershberger, Apple Creek, OH
  Mrs. David Kurtz, Smicksburg, PA

Cold and Flu Tea

1 tablespoon apple cider vinegar
1 tablespoon honey
1 tablespoon lemon
juice (optional)
½ to 1 cup warm water

Mix all ingredients and drink in the morning.

Clara Yoder, Sugar Grove, PA

Make it hot and sip slowly to soothe colds.

Mrs. Levi J. Stutzman, West Salem, OH

Mama's Red Raspberry Brew

½ gallon raspberry leaves
3 cups alfalfa herb
3 cups peppermint leaves

2 cups nettle leaves
Honey to taste

Blend first four ingredients. To make tea, add 2 to 3 teaspoons mixed herbs to 1 cup boiling water. Steep 2 to 3 minutes. Strain and add honey to taste.

ANNA ZOOK, DALTON, OH

Catnip Tea

Catnip tea can be grown in your garden. Make this tea before it blooms. Cut off about 5 to 6 stems with leaves. Dry and use later or use it fresh. It may be used as a healthy tea, or it can be used as a soak for sore muscles or sprains. Soak any part of your body in heated water with the tea leaves. Heat the water again and soak for up to 4 times a day. It also helps with cellulitis; place the tea leaves on that part of your body while you are soaking.

DIANNA YODER, GOSHEN, IN

Corn Silk Tea

Corn silk is good for making tea. Drinking it can help with kidney infections and bladder infections.

DIANNA YODER, GOSHEN, IN

Ginger Tea

1 tablespoon freshly grated ginger
1 slice lemon

1 teaspoon honey
8 ounces boiling water

Steep ginger, lemon, and honey in water for several minutes. Strain and drink. This is a great immune booster and flu fighter.

EMMA MILLER, BALTIC, OH

Lemon Tea

Squeezing a lemon wedge into your tea turns your drink into a powerful superfood. Lemon increases the level of available antioxidants in the tea. Antioxidants found in white, green, and black tea are more powerful than vitamins C and E in terms of stopping cell damage. And they lower cholesterol levels.

ESTHER MARTIN, FLEETWOOD, PA

MINT TEA

Boil fresh mint in water until water turns dark green. Strain out the mint and store the water in a quart jar in the refrigerator. Dilute in a little water and take for headache, stomachache, cramps, and general malaise. For children, add a little honey.

PARSLEY TEA

For sluggish kidneys and bladder, drink a tea made of parsley.

MRS. JOSEP MILLER, NAVARRE, OH

THYME TEA

Add 1 teaspoon dried thyme to 1 cup boiling water. Cover and let steep for 20 to 30 minutes. Strain and drink. Thyme heals upper respiratory infections like bronchitis and whooping cough. Thyme is a powerful antiseptic.

MRS. MARTHA BYLER, ATLANTIC, PA

The seeds of discouragement will not grow in a thankful heart.

*God owes us nothing,
but He gives us
everything.*

Super Tonic

Hot peppers	Ginger root
Garlic cloves	Horseradish
Onions	Apple cider vinegar

Use equal parts hot pepper, garlic, and onion (e.g., a pound each). Use only half as much ginger and horseradish (e.g., a half pound each). Grind up all ingredients and cover with apple cider vinegar. Stir every day for 2 weeks. Strain. Bottle and use for colds and coughs. Take by spoonful morning and evening. Take extra as needed. Dilute with water for children.

MRS. AMOS B. EICHER, MONROE, IN

pH Balance

| 1 teaspoon apple cider vinegar | 1 teaspoon honey |
| 1 teaspoon lemon juice | |

Combine vinegar, lemon juice, and honey in a cup. Fill with warm water. Drink this before breakfast. Helps balance pH in the body and can even help with weight loss.

AARON AND EMMA GINGERICH, BREMAN, OH

Hay-Time Switchel

Thought to originate in the West Indies during the 1600s, switchel made its way to the American colonies and became a popular drink to revive thirsty farmers.

2 cups sugar	1 teaspoon ground ginger
1 cup molasses	1 gallon water, divided
¼ cup apple cider vinegar	

Heat sugar, molasses, vinegar, and ginger in 1 quart water until dissolved. Add remaining water, chill, and serve. Yields 1 gallon.

MOLLIE STOLZFUS, CHARLOTTE HALL, MD

Replenishment Drink

1 teaspoon ginger
2 tablespoons vinegar

½ cup sugar
1 quart water

Mix and serve over ice. Refreshing for when you have been working out in the heat.

Emma Byler, New Wilmington, PA

Electrolyte Drink

1 pint water
1 pint blackberry juice
½ teaspoon salt

1 teaspoon baking soda
3 tablespoons sorghum
  molasses or honey

Combine all ingredients and serve warm or cold. We find this refreshing and energizing after a bout of fever or stomach disorders.

K. Hertzler, West Salisbury, PA

Jogging in a Jug

1 part apple cider vinegar
1 part grape juice
5 parts apple juice

Mix ingredients and take 2 ounces per day. Take faithfully for 3 months before you'll notice a difference. This is good for high cholesterol. It helps clean out your arteries and relieves arthritis.

Emma Byler, New Wilmington, PA
Malinda M. Gingerich, Spartansburg, PA

*The best reason for doing
what's right today
is tomorrow.*

Natural Detoxing and Energizing Drink

12 to 16 ounces warm water
2 tablespoons apple cider vinegar
2 tablespoons lemon juice
½ to 1 teaspoon ground ginger

¼ teaspoon cinnamon
Dash cayenne pepper
1 teaspoon raw honey

Combine all ingredients and drink warm or cold. If you are looking for an easy way to cleanse your body and boost your energy, have this drink once a day before breakfast or lunch. For more intense detoxification, drink it 3 times per day 20 minutes before meals for 2 weeks.

IVA YODER, GOSHEN, IN

Homemade Pedialyte

1 pint water
Juice from 1 whole
　lemon or orange

½ teaspoon baking soda
2 tablespoons sugar
Pinch salt

Stir all ingredients until sugar dissolves. This drink will help keep child or adult from dehydrating when they cannot keep anything down. Give child 1 teaspoon every 15 minutes. If you give more, the child will throw it up. A teaspoon is enough only to wet the tongue and won't cause stomach upset.

KATHRYN TROYER, RUTHERFORD, TN

Homemade Gatorade/Pedialyte (*Rehydration Fluid*)

¼ cup fresh lemon juice
¼ cup maple syrup
½ teaspoon unrefined salt

1 quart water (or replace half water with coconut water or grape juice)
Mix all together well. To rehydrate infants, give a dropperful every 2 to 3 minutes.

LYDIA MILLER, LOUDONVILLE, OH

Remedy for Lengthy Stomach Bug

28 ounces Gatorade
1 teaspoon sugar
½ teaspoon salt

Fill an empty 28-ounce Gatorade bottle with half water and half Gatorade. Add sugar and salt. Cap the bottle and shake until sugar and salt dissolve.

This recipe was given to us by a doctor when one of our boys had flu and diarrhea for 2 weeks. It is okay to give to small children so they don't dehydrate when sick.

EMMA A. HERSHBERGER, APPLE CREEK, OH

Cold and Sore Throat Remedy

1 cup boiling water	2 tablespoons honey
1½ teaspoons salt	1 cup apple cider vinegar
2 teaspoons red pepper	

Pour boiling water into quart jar or pan with lid. Add salt, red pepper, and honey. Cover with lid and let cool. Shake or stir mixture well several times. Add vinegar. Always shake or stir well before using. Take 1 teaspoonful as often as you wish.

Mrs. Samuel Lee, Plymouth, IL

Sore Throat Sipper

1 teaspoon apple cider vinegar	Dash black pepper
1 teaspoon salt	½ glass warm water

Mix all ingredients and sip. Also works on fever.

Malinda M. Gingerich, Spartansburg, PA .

Tea for Cough and Runny Nose

Mix equal amounts of dried chamomile leaves and dried oregano. Add 1 teaspoon dried mixture to 1 cup boiling water. Let steep 5 minutes, strain, and drink.

Kathryn Troyer, Rutherford, TN

Drink for Cold and Flu

2 egg whites, beaten	Dash nutmeg (optional)
2 tablespoons white sugar	1 pint lukewarm water

Stir together and sip often. It can cure the worst cases of cold and flu in a short time.

Emma Byler, New Wilmington, PA

Drink it, and you will be surprised at how soon a fever will be gone.

Mrs. Carlisle Schmidt, Carlisle, KY

Cough Remedy Tea

1 part thyme leaves	1 part peppermint leaves
1 part plantain leaves	Equal parts vodka and glycerin

Mix herbs and fill a glass jar half full with herbs. Mix vodka and glycerin. Fill jar with liquid mixture. Let sit for 6 weeks and shake daily. Strain and bottle.

Tea:

Use ½ teaspoon herb tincture per cup of hot water. Sip a cup several times a day. If given promptly and often, coughs (whooping, bronchial, asthma, and pneumonia) will usually not stand a chance.

William and Rebecca Troyer, Navarre, OH

You are never fully dressed in the morning until you put on a smile.

When hemmed in on all sides,
the only place to look is up.

Soothing Cough Syrup

3 cups water
3 tablespoons honey
3 large cloves garlic
1 tablespoon fenugreek seed

Put all ingredients in saucepan and boil until it reduces down to ½ cup syrup. Take 1 teaspoonful as needed.

K. Hertzler, West Salisbury, PA

Cough Syrup for Whooping Cough

1 lemon, thinly sliced
1 cup flaxseed
1 quart water
2 ounces honey

In saucepan simmer lemon, flaxseed, and water for 4 hours. Do not boil. Strain while hot and add honey. Pour into pint jar and fill with water.

Use as soon as cough is noticeable. Dose 1 tablespoon 4 times per day. Add an additional dose after each severe fit of coughing. This remedy has never failed me, bringing about a cure in 4 to 5 days.

Emme D. Byler, New Wilmington, PA

Cough Syrup

½ cup apple cider vinegar
½ cup water
1 teaspoon cayenne pepper
3 tablespoons honey

Mix all ingredients well. Administer by teaspoonfuls. This is also good for sore throats.

Mary and Katie Yoder, Goshen, IN

WHOOPING COUGH REMEDY

Put 3 or 4 chestnut leaves in 2 cups boiling water. Steep several minutes. Strain and sweeten with honey. Let children drink some 5 or 6 times a day.

MATTIE PETERSHEIM, JUNCTION CITY, OH
MARY H. STUTZMAN, GILMAN, WI

WHOOPING COUGH SYRUP

1 lemon, thinly sliced	1 quart water
1 cup flaxseed	2 ounces honey

In saucepan simmer lemon, flaxseed, and water for 4 hours. Do not boil. You may need to add more water when cool. Strain while hot. Add honey. Measure; if less than 2 cups, add water. Give 1 tablespoon every 4 hours or as needed.

EMMA BEILER, DELTA, PA

This works well to dispel mucous. Take some after every coughing spell up to a cup per day. Great for whooping cough or any other lingering cough.

LYDIA RUTH BYER, NEWBURG, PA
EMMA A. HERSHBERGER, APPLE CREEK, OH

This remedy has never been known to fail me. Effective for curing cough in children in 4 to 5 days if given before first whoops begin.

ROSINA SCHWARTZ, SALEM, IN
MARY H. STUTZMAN, GILMAN, WI

Experience is a hard teacher. She gives the test first and the lesson afterward.

KIDNEY STONE REMEDY

6 red beets
3 quarts water

Clean and wash beets (don't peel or slice). Combine beets and 3 quarts water in kettle. Boil slowly so as not to boil the water away. After 1 hour, strain the water into a jar and store in a cool place so remedy won't sour. Drink 3 glasses a day until gone. Almost never is a second dose necessary. The kidney stones don't pass; they just melt away.

IDA MILLER, MEDFORD, WI

RED BEET TONIC

When you are canning beets, use plenty of water as you cook beets. Strain off water. Add:

2 gallons water
14½ pounds sugar

4 slices whole wheat bread
4 cakes or tablespoons dry yeast

Put beet water and water in large crock or pail. Stir in sugar. Toast bread and spread 1 tablespoon yeast on each slice. Flip yeast side down on top of beet water. Cover container with white 100 percent cotton cloth. Let stand for 3 weeks. Strain and bottle liquid.

Use 1 tablespoon tonic 2 to 3 times a day for blood tonic or purifier. We also like to use it at start of stomach flu or upset.

Recipe may be cut in half for a smaller batch.

Tonic will keep for more than a year.

LYDIA HERSHBERGER, DALTON, OH
LIZZIE H. STUTZMAN, GILMAN, WI

BLOOD TONIC

6 lemons
6 oranges
6 grapefruit

4 tablespoons Epsom salt
1 quart boiling water

Grind up lemons, oranges, and grapefruit, including rinds. Sprinkle ground citrus with Epsom salt. Cover with boiling water. Let stand overnight. Next morning, strain through cloth bag and press out juice. Take 1 tablespoon 3 times a day. Keep in cool place as it will spoil. Can reduce size of batch.

MARY H. STUTZMAN, GILMAN, WI

CANCER TONIC

1 quart water	1 tablespoon ginger
1 cup bloodroot	1 pint quality whiskey
2 cups clover blossoms	

Bring water to boil and add bloodroot, clover blossoms, and ginger. Boil down to 1 pint. Strain. Add liquid to whiskey. Take a teaspoonful 3 times a day.

MARY H. STUTZMAN, GILMAN, WI

GALLSTONE FLUSH

Eat a light breakfast (e.g., a piece of dry toast and a cup of tea). Drink 1 gallon apple juice from morning until 3:00 p.m. Stop drinking at 3:00 p.m. even if juice still remains. Consume nothing else before bedtime. Squeeze lemons to make ½ cup fresh juice; put in pint jar. Add ½ cup olive oil. Put on lid and shake until thoroughly mixed. Drink all at once just before retiring to bed. Lie on your right side as long as comfortable.

ELAM AND SARAH BEILER, DOYLESBURG, PA

WHAT CANCER CANNOT DO

It cannot cripple love.
It cannot shatter hope.
It cannot corrode faith.
It cannot destroy peace.
It cannot kill friendship.
It cannot suppress memories.
It cannot silence courage.
It cannot invade the soul.
It cannot steal eternal life.
It cannot conquer the spirit.

DAVID AND LAURA BYLER,
NEW CASTLE, PA

FIRST AID TIPS and OINTMENTS

BEE STING REMEDIES

- Put honey on bee stings. Or make paste with baking soda and water. Coat sting and let dry.

  BETHANY MARTIN, HOMER CITY, PA

- Mix equal parts baking soda and vinegar to put on sting. Works very well.

  EMMA BYLER, NEW WILMINGTON, PA
  ANNA KING, NEW CASTLE, IN

- For relief of bee stings, get a leaf of plantain (pig's ear). Rub the leaf on the sting until it quits hurting. Also keeps it from swelling. These leaves can often be found in your own yard.

  MRS. JOSEP MILLER, NAVARRE, OH
  MRS. JOSEPH SCHWARTZ, BERNE, IN

INSECT BITE REMEDIES

- For insect bite, apply slice of raw onion on area.

  EMMA BYLER, NEW WILMINGTON, PA

- Apply apple cider vinegar full strength to insect bites to relieve the sting and itching.

  DAVID AND LAURA BYLER, NEW CASTLE, PA

Mosquito Bite Remedies

- Moisten bar of soap and rub on bite. It will relieve itching and act as disinfectant to prevent infection.

  Mattie Petersheim, Junction City, OH

- Rub the inside of a banana peel over mosquito and other insect bites to reduce swelling and irritation. Also works for small burns to help keep from getting infected.

  Mary Miller, Belmopan, Belize, South America

Snakebite

Gently rub a layer of 100 percent pure cold-pressed castor oil on and around the swollen area to help relieve pain and aching. If venomous snake, seek medical immediately.

Malinda M. Gingerich, Spartansburg, PA

Itchy Ears

For itchy ears, dip a cotton swab into a solution of 1 tablespoon vinegar and 3 tablespoons water and carefully clean inside of ears.

Nathan and Anna Fisher, Salisbury, PA

Daily prayers are the best remedies for daily cares.

Earache Remedies

- Rub vapor chest rub or other salve, in front of the ears and right behind them all the way down the neck. Use firm pressure but not too hard for young ones. Always rub down and not upward. Also rub salve beneath the jawbone, starting beneath the ear and working forward to the chin. Do this several times. Good for sore throat as well.

  Mrs. Samuel Lee, Plymouth, IL

- Finely chop onion. Place onion on square cloth such as handkerchief. Bring up corners and twist cloth around onion. Keep twisting and squeezing until you have enough juice to put a few drops in aching ear. It's that simple and really does work. I like to warm the drops a little. You can also put a warm bag of rice over the ear after applying drops.

  Martha Troyer, Millersburg, OH

- Mix 2 tablespoons olive oil and 2 freshly minced garlic buds. Let sit a day or two. Strain and use as eardrops for earaches.

  Kate Bontrager, Middlebury, IN

- Put 1 drop garlic oil and 2 drops lobella in ear twice a day. Plug ear with cotton.

  Mrs. Henry A. Swartzentruber, Liberty, KY

- Use equal parts white vinegar and rubbing alcohol for earache. Warm the mixture slightly and put several drops in ear as needed.

  Lovina D. Gingerich, Mount Ayr, IA

Remedy for Swimmer's Ear

Combine equal parts rubbing alcohol and white vinegar in a small bottle. Put 2 or 3 drops in ears before and after swimming. The alcohol dries out the ear, and the vinegar acts as an antibacterial agent. A slight pull on the earlobe will be painful to someone who has swimmer's ear.

Prevention hint: After being underwater, tip your head to the side to clear water out of the ears.

Emma Fisher, Ronks, PA

Ear Oil

8 cloves garlic, minced fine
2 tablespoons mullein
Olive oil

Place garlic and mullein in double boiler and just cover with olive oil. Keep mixture hot for 2 hours. Do not boil. Strain into glass jar and store in refrigerator. To use, warm and drop 2 drops into infected ear. Will usually dry up fluid behind eardrum or cure ear infection if used regularly.

Mrs. Kristina Byler, Crab Orchard, KY

Green Salve

⅓ part comfrey leaves	Wax
⅓ part calendula flowers	Vitamin E oil capsules
⅓ part plantain	Chamomile, lavender,
Olive oil	or tea tree oil

Put comfrey, calendula, and plantain in jar. Cover with olive oil. Seal jar. Place jar in paper bag and set in sun for 2 to 6 weeks. Strain and press herbs to capture every bit of oil. Measure oil. For every ounce of oil, add 1 tablespoon grated wax and 1 capsule vitamin E oil. Add a few drops of chamomile, lavender, or tea tree oil for scent.

This is a mighty all-purpose salve. Very good for diaper rash, cuts, dry hands, and more.

LYDIA RUTH BYER, NEWBURG, PA

Marigold Salve

- Heat 2 pints olive oil in a skillet until you see shimmering heat waves. Put in as many marigold blossoms as you can easily fit into the skillet. Fry until blossoms start to brown oil and melt. Keep stirring as it cools. This salve relieves pain from cuts and burns fast.

MALINDA M. GINGERICH, SPARTANSBURG, PA

- Add 3 ounces beeswax to oil, stirring as it cools. This is a very useful salve to keep on hand for most any ailment.

LINDA MILLER, SPARTANSBURG, PA

Painful Burn Tips

- Mix equal parts castor oil and cod liver oil. Soak cotton ball or cloth with mixture and lay it on burn. Cotton is said to be better than gauze. Relieves pain quickly.
- Vaseline is said to stop pain in burns almost immediately.
- Dip burned hand in cold, fresh-skimmed cream or top milk to relieve pain.
- Puncture a vitamin E capsule and put pure oil directly on burn or other sore. Heals burns quickly and prevents scars.

LIZZIE H. STUTZMAN, GILMAN, WI

Burn Remedy

If you burn your finger or hand, plunge it into flour. Some people keep some flour in freezer to use on burns.

BETHANY MARTIN, HOMER CITY, PA

GREASE BURN

When using bacon or hot grease, if it splatters, apply honey often on your red spots to prevent them from blistering.

KATIE W. YODER, GOSHEN, IN

SALVE FOR BURNS

1 gram alum   2 egg whites
1 cup lard

Mix alum into lard. Add egg whites and mix thoroughly. Very effective for large burns. Spread on cloth and cover burn area. Also good for sunburns. Keep in small containers in freezer to have ready when needed.

MRS. SAMUEL LEE, PLYMOUTH, IL

SUNBURN REMEDY

- Put apple cider vinegar on sunburns that have not blistered. Will prevent peeling if applied immediatcly after exposure.

BETHANY MARTIN, HOMER CITY, PA
BARBARA E. YODER, GILMAN, WI

- For sunburn relief, use aloe vera gel straight from the plant.

SUSIE MILLER, DUNDEE, OH

RASH

We have had good results with pure olive oil for any hurting rash behind ears, under arms, and also baby's diaper rash. The olive oil is very soothing and healing.

MRS. HENRY A. SWARTZENTRUBER, LIBERTY, KY

POISON IVY REMEDIES

- We use olive oil on poison ivy, nothing else unless we wash the rash with vinegar water. We have good results with that.

MRS. HENRY A. SWARTZENTRUBER, LIBERTY, KY

- Drinking sassafras and burdock tea is good to get rid of poison ivy.

MARTHA MILLER, EDGAR, WI

- Rub inside of banana peel on itchy area.

SADIE FISHER, AARONSBURG, PA

POISON IVY MEDICINE

2 tablespoons Borax   1 pint hot water
2 tablespoons powdered alum

Mix; then dip cotton in the mixture and put on rash.

SADIE FISHER, AARONSBURG, PA

Bumps and Bruises

Arnica is a must-have for our first aid shelf. Rub arnica tincture on bumps to heal them quicker and prevent black-and-blue bruises. It is also a great pain reliever.

LEVI AND MARY MILLER, JUNCTION CITY, OH

Soak for Cuts and Scrapes

For cuts and scrapes, put 1 tablespoon wood ash in 1 quart hot water and brew like tea. Add cold water until comfortable to soak the wound for 30 minutes, more or less.

MRS. LEVI J. STUTZMAN, WEST SALEM, OH

Bleeding Cuts

To stop small cuts from bleeding, dust with cayenne pepper. Works well and will not burn a fresh cut. For a cut that won't stop bleeding, cover it with honey and wrap with a bandage such as strips of a white sheet.

BARBARA E. YODER, GILMAN, WI

Bleeding

One time my husband got a small hammer chip in his arm, and we couldn't stop the bleeding until we put baking soda on it. Then we bandaged it with the soda still on. Cayenne pepper did not work that time. It was just a pinpoint hole. We thought it might have hit the vein as it bled so much.

MRS. HENRY A. SWARTZENTRUBER, LIBERTY, KY

Cut Remedy

Use the skin (the layer just inside the shell) of a raw egg to put over cuts to hold them together. Leave it on until it peels off by itself.

EMMA BEILER, DELTA, PA

People can't stumble when they are on their knees.

Drawing Agent

To draw infection from a sore, stir a teaspoon of salt into an egg yolk. Apply to sore and cover with cloth.

Lizzie H. Stutzman, Gilman, WI

Infected Area Remedy

Mix charcoal and ground flaxseed with castor oil to form a spreadable paste. To pull glass, dirt, or other particle from skin sore, apply mixture to sore area.

Lena Troyer, Redding, IA

Sore Remedy

Scrape a potato finely and tie pulp over sore. It is said to heal when all other remedies have failed.

Lizzie H. Stutzman, Gilman, WI

Open Sore Remedy

Set up two dishpans. In first pan, place ¼ cup Epsom salt in 1 gallon hot water (120 degrees). In second pan, place ¼ cup Epsom salt in 1 gallon water with ice cubes.

Use two white Turkish towels. Soak one in hot water and wrap around sore (generally used on arms or legs) for 3 minutes. Remove and wrap cold water–soaked towel around sore for 2 minutes. Repeat hot soak. Always start and end with hot soak. Do this process morning and evening. Dress sore with B&W (burn and wound) ointment and burdock in between.

Rebecca E. Stutzman, Gilman, WI

Wounds

Red beets are very good to put on punctured wounds or sores. Also on swollen knees or sprains. Wash and grate red beets and put them on infected areas. Cover with gauze or a towel and put plastic wrap around it. Redress several times until wound is better.

Sadie Fisher, Aaronsburg, PA

Splinters

For splinters, apply Union black salve and a bandage. Leave it overnight. The next day the splinter should remove easily.

Miriam Byler, Spartansburg, PA

Pinched Fingers and Toes

Wrap pinched area in fresh plantain leaves from your lawn. When I got my finger caught in the washing machine wringer, I put some crushed plantain leaves on my finger, and the throbbing soon stopped.

Lena Troyer, Redding, IA

Corn and Sore Remedy

Dip cotton ball in peppermint oil and tape over corn or sore. Leave on 3 to 4 days; then soak area in warm water. Repeat as necessary.

Lizzie H. Stutzman, Gilman, WI

Wart Remedy

- For warts, soak a bandage or cotton ball in apple cider vinegar and secure over wart. Do this for 4 to 7 days or until wart falls off. If it comes back, you probably didn't leave the bandage on long enough. The first 1 to 3 times this procedure can hurt, but after that it doesn't. You don't have to leave it on the whole night if it hurts, and I've even skipped a night and still get good results.

Miriam Byler, Spartansburg, PA

- My experience with warts was when I was a girl I had warts on my fingers. All I used was hydrogen peroxide. Just put it on the warts a couple times a day. No need to bandage it.

Mrs. Henry A. Swartzentruber, Liberty, KY

Every tomorrow has two handles. We can grasp the handle of anxiety or the handle of faith.

Mouth Sore Remedy

Moisten finger and dip into powdered alum. Place alum on sore. Hold in mouth awhile then spit it out. Sores heal fast with this remedy.

BETHANY MARTIN, HOMER CITY, PA

Toothache Remedy

- Beat together 1 egg white and 1 teaspoon black pepper. Rub on outside of cheek over painful area.

  EMMA A. HERSHBERGER, APPLE CREEK, OH

- To stop toothache, soak cotton in ammonia and apply to aching tooth.

  MATTIE PETERSHEIM, JUNCTION CITY, OH

- For a toothache, swish Dental Health around your teeth every hour until toothache subsides; then use once or twice a day for maintenance.
- For toothache or abscess, we have had good results with putting 1 drop Dental Health on affected spot. Be careful, though—it is strong. It might be best to dilute the oil in pure olive oil.

  MIRIAM BYLER, SPARTANSBURG, PA

- Mix together equal parts red pepper, chaparral, and white willow bark powders. Put into capsules or mix into water or juice. Take until you get relief.

  RACHEL MILLER, MILLERSBURG, OH

- To get rid of toothache, put Swedish bitters on tooth.

  MRS. JOSEPH SCHWARTZ, BERNE, IN

Sore Tongue

I think a white tongue that gets sore, comes from too much bad bacteria. Sugar feeds bacteria, so avoiding sugary drinks and a lot of sweet treats greatly helps. Also, use baking soda to brush your teeth and tongue.

MIRIAM BYLER, SPARTANSBURG, PA

Pink Eye

Hold a warm, damp tea bag on the infected eye.

NATHAN AND ANNA FISHER, SALISBURY, PA

Respiratory Aids

Stuffy Nose Remedies

- If your children have stuffy noses during the night, put drops of peppermint oil on their pillows. Try to put it to the sides where skin won't touch, as it can burn the cheeks a little. You can also use other oil blends for better breathing.
- Another remedy for stuffy noses is to put peppermint or other oils good for respiratory issues into a diffuser. Put the diffuser by the child's bed if needed.
- Also for stuffy noses, dilute peppermint or other oil blend for respiratory issues with carrier oil and put in a roller bottle. Rub on nose and around ears, neck, and so on.

Miriam Byler, Spartansburg, PA

- Put a few drops of peppermint oil in a cup of warm water. Breathe in the vapors. Then you may also drink it.

Bertha Schwartz, Monroe, IN

Cold Remedy

Dice medium onion into pint jar. Add 1 teaspoon brown sugar. Let stand for 1 hour before using. Give 2 to 3 teaspoonfuls to children every hour.

Emma Byler, New Wilmington, PA

Chest Cold Remedy

2 teaspoons red pepper	2 tablespoons flour
2 teaspoons dry mustard	½ cup lard
2 teaspoons baking soda	

Combine all ingredients. Put some in a cloth, fold, and pin on nightclothes over the chest. Leave overnight.

Rebecca E. Stutzman, Gilman, WI

COLD OR PNEUMONIA REMEDY

In saucepan, heat 2 tablespoons lard, 2 tablespoons kerosene, and 2 tablespoons turpentine until fat melts and is hot to touch. Rub warm mixture on back and chest. Soak small cloth in mixture and put on chest. Cover with warm flannel.

MATTIE PETERSHEIM, JUNCTION CITY, OH

COUGH POULTICE

1 teaspoon cinnamon	½ teaspoon ginger
1 teaspoon allspice	1 teaspoon dry mustard
1 teaspoon nutmeg	Lard

Mix spices and work in enough lard to make a paste. Spread on throat and/or chest.

MARY STUTZMAN, WEST SALEM, OH

SORE THROAT REMEDIES

- Mix vinegar with strong dash of salt and red or black pepper. Gargle with it often.

BARBARA E. YODER, GILMAN, WI

- Put 1 teaspoon vinegar in a cup of warm water. Add ½ teaspoon honey. Gargle or sip slowly. We also have good results with using a small amount of horehound oil in the back of the mouth.

MRS. HENRY A. SWARTZENTRUBER, LIBERTY, KY

- For sore throat, dissolve ½ teaspoon salt in ¾ cup hot water and gargle several times.

SORE THROAT WRAPS

- Soak a standard pillowcase in cold water. Wring out and wrap around neck. Cover cold wrap with dry flannel pillowcase. Go to bed and rest. The coldness draws out the pain.

EMMA MILLER, BALTIC, OH

- Red beets can be used for sore throat. Slice the beets and put them on your neck. Wrap a cloth around the beets to hold them in place.

DIANNA YODER, GOSHEN, IN

PNEUMONIA SALVE

3½ cups fresh lard
6 ounces beeswax
2 tablespoons menthol crystals

2 tablespoons pure gum
   spirits of turpentine
2 ounces camphor essential oil
2 ounces eucalyptus essential oil

Melt lard and beeswax over low heat. Add menthol crystals. When dissolved, remove from heat and let sit a couple minutes. Add turpentine and stir; then add essential oils. Pour into jars.

To use: Rub on chest, back, and bottoms of feet for colds and coughs. I like to cover chest and back with a warm cloth and put thick socks on feet. The salve works well to keep cough loose and makes breathing easier.

MALINDA M. GINGERICH, SPARTANSBURG, PA

CHEST RUB

Mix equal parts household ammonia, turpentine, and castor oil. Rub on chest and back. Cover with warm cloth. This will not blister, so you can put it on heavily, and it can be used on babies and children. In severe cases, repeat every 2 to 3 hours. Never fails me for bronchitis, chest tightness, or pneumonia.

EMMA A. HERSHBERGER, APPLE CREEK, OH

Rub on chest, back, neck, throat, and bottoms of feet for colds, RSV, and the like.

LEVI AND MARY MILLER, JUNCTION CITY, OH

HOMEMADE VICKS RUB

½ gallon virgin olive oil
4 ounces beeswax
3 teaspoons camphor essential oil
3 teaspoons eucalyptus
   essential oil

2½ ounces menthol crystals
   (use less if you don't
   want it as strong)

Heat olive oil to rippling. Add beeswax. When beeswax is melted, turn off heat and add essential oils and menthol crystals. Stir until warm. Ladle into jars.

(Menthol crystals are a by-product of the manufacturing of mint essential oil, used for soothing and calming effect.)

MALINDA M. GINGERICH, SPARTANSBURG, PA

HOMEMADE CHEST RUB

¼ cup coconut oil
8 to 10 drops eucalyptus
   essential oil

8 to 10 drops lemon essential oil
8 to 10 drops peppermint
   essential oil

Stir all together; mix well. Store in glass jar (lemon oil breaks down plastic). Rub a bit on the chest and neck at first sign of a cold.

KATURAH MILLER, LOUDONVILLE, OH

Grandma's Lung Fever Salve

3 pounds lard
2 packages Red Man tobacco
1 pound raisins

4 medium onions, chopped
2 teaspoons camphor

Melt lard. Add tobacco, raisins, and onions. Boil slowly at least 30 minutes. Add camphor. When melted, strain and put into jars. When needed, rub on chest and back. Cover with thick, warm cloth. Can be used for pneumonia. Safe on babies.

Mrs. Samuel Lee, Plymouth, IL

Garlic Salve

⅓ cup coconut oil
2 tablespoons olive oil

8 cloves garlic, peeled
5 drops lavender oil (optional)

In blender blend all ingredients on high speed. Can be strained to remove garlic pieces. Stores in refrigerator for a long time.

Use on chest and bottom of feet for colds, coughs, respiratory syncytial virus (RSV), and pneumonia. For earaches, place salve on cotton swab and rub around ear.

Ruth Hochstetler, Dundee, OH

I like to add several drops of frankincense oil.

Linda Miller, Spartansburg, PA
Rebecca E. Stutzman, Gilman, WI

The one thing worse than a quitter is the person who is afraid to start.

Vinegar for Chest Congestion or Cold

Put cider vinegar on a cloth. Place cloth on chest for 2 hours.

Marilyn Hostetler, Topeka, IN

Chest Congestion

For chest congestion, rub chest and back thoroughly with Unker's therapeutic rub or eucalyptus oil, then cover with a warm flannel cloth. Also rub some on the bottom of feet and put on warm socks. Do that at least 3 to 4 times a day.

Mrs. Daniel Wickey, Berne, IN

Chest Congestion Advice

For tightness in chest, mix equal parts turpentine and olive oil and rub liberally on chest, back, stomach, and bottoms of feet. Cover with a warm cloth. I heat cotton diapers on the stove as hot as can be tolerated and put them on the chest and back.

For severe tightness, do this as often as 4 times a day, especially at bedtime. For babies, it can be done more often, but dilute the turpentine with more olive oil.

I have also used garlic salves, Unker's therapeutic rub, or other salves with good results. But I think any salve works best if you cover it with a very warm cloth. If it doesn't work, maybe you aren't putting the salve on liberally enough.

Another remedy for tightness in the chest of a child is to heat a teakettle of water until it is boiling very hard. Set it on the floor in a safe place, then sit near it with your child and cover yourself and the child and the kettle with a sheet. Take the lid off and let the steam out. You can add Unker's or peppermint oil to the water for older children, but babies cannot breathe if vapors are too strong. Have the house warm so that they don't get chilled when they come out from under the sheet as they'll be sweaty.

You can also "steam" a baby by wetting a sheet with hot water, wringing it out, and spreading it over their crib.

I have found steaming methods to be helpful for a sore, dry throat.

Miriam Byler, Spartansburg, PA

Onion Poultice

Chop or thinly slice a few onions. Put in saucepan with 2 to 3 tablespoons lard and fry until slightly browned. Remove from heat and add 1 or 2 tablespoons apple cider vinegar and enough cornmeal to make a poultice. Don't make it too dry. Put mixture between two old rags and cover or fold up edges. Put it on chest overnight or use immediately if needed. This is a remedy to try before going to the doctor for chest colds or coughs. If one application doesn't work, try again.

EMMA BEILER, DELTA, PA

Onion Poultice for Severe Coughs

Slice or chop 10 large onions and put in a large frying pan. Cover with vinegar. Simmer until onions are soft. Add enough flour to make a paste. I put the mixture on a soft cloth and apply to the chest and back as hot as the patient can tolerate. Keep reheating the poultice until patient starts perspiring on chest. Do not leave on children for too long as this is very strong, but it does work great.

MALINDA M. GINGERICH, SPARTANSBURG, PA

Onion Plaster for Croup

1 to 2 heaping tablespoons lard
1 medium onion, chopped

1 to 2 tablespoons apple
  cider vinegar
Cornmeal

Melt lard in a pan and add onion. Cook over medium heat until onion becomes translucent. Take off heat and add vinegar and enough cornmeal to make a nice paste, but not too thick. Put paste in an old sock and lay it on chest.

IDA BYLER, FRAZEYSBURG, OH
SADIE BYLER, FRAZEYSBURG, OH

*The glory of tomorrow is rooted
in the drudgery of today.*

Pneumonia Poultice

Shave flakes off bar of homemade soap. Add to hot water to make paste. Stir in bran or whole wheat flour to thicken it. (Bran like that fed to livestock works.) Make a poultice. Put it on chest as hot as can be tolerated. We have used it for all ages, from babies to the elderly.

MARY STUTZMAN, WEST SALEM, OH

Pneumonia or Flu Foot Soak

1 to 2 tablespoons dry mustard   1 to 2 teaspoons cayenne pepper
1 to 2 teaspoons ginger

Mix all in pail of hot water and soak feet for 15 to 20 minutes.

MRS. MARTHA BYLER, ATLANTIC, PA

Pineapple Juice

Drink pineapple juice to loosen coughs. It also helps reduce swelling of the sinuses.

MALINDA M. GINGERICH, SPARTANSBURG, PA

Sinus Infection

For sinus infections, colds, and the like, take 5 to 10 garlic pills every couple of hours as soon as you feel sickness starting.

MIRIAM BYLER, SPARTANSBURG, PA

Virus Remedy

Drop diluted oregano essential oil in carrier oil, spread along spine, and rub in well.

KATHRYN TROYER, RUTHERFORD, TN

Success is when you get what you want.
Happiness is when you want what you get

OTHER HEALTH ADVICE

ACID RELIEF

Mix 2 tablespoons apple cider vinegar with 1 pint water. Sip throughout the day. Will change your acid to alkaline for relief.

MALINDA M. GINGERICH, SPARTANSBURG, PA

HEADACHE RELIEF

- For a headache, I have good results with putting a few drops of peppermint oil in a half glass of warm water and drinking it. Sometimes it helps to put peppermint oil on your temples.

MRS. HENRY A. SWARTZENTRUBER, LIBERTY, KY

- Eat 10 to 12 almonds to equal 2 aspirins for a migraine headache.

RACHEL MILLER, MILLERSBURG, OH

FAINTING (DIZZY SPELLS)

A drink of vinegar is a sure cure for fainting.

BARBARA HERSHBERGER, FREDERICKSBURG, OH

BARBARA E. YODER, GILMAN, WI

HICCUPS

For hiccups, take a spoonful of peanut butter.

MIRIAM BYLER, SPARTANSBURG, PA

Dehydration Remedy

Rub young children with warm olive oil on back and belly until skin doesn't absorb any more. Supposedly this feeds them through the skin, preventing dehydration.

SALOMA YODER, MERCER, MO

Colitis or Stomach Remedy

Carefully take a cupful of red-hot charcoal from burned wood and put into 2 cups boiling water. Strain. Sip liquid throughout the day. May be repeated 2 to 3 days later.

MATTIE PETERSHEIM, JUNCTION CITY, OH

Remedy for Upset Stomach

2 cups water	2 tablespoons honey or sugar
¼ teaspoon baking soda	¼ cup orange juice

Mix all ingredients in blender. Take 1 tablespoon every half hour or as tolerated. Take right away after vomiting if possible.

MRS. JOHN BEACHY, MOUNT VICTORY, OH

Stomach Upset

To settle your stomach, cook 1 tablespoon dry rice in 2 cups water for 20 minutes. Strain and add enough water to the strained liquid to make 2 cups. Sip slowly until upset is gone.

DAVID AND LAURA BYLER, NEW CASTLE, PA

Food Poisoning

- If you suspect food poisoning, drink 2 tablespoons apple cider vinegar. Or take some for prevention if you go to carry-in dinners or other places where there is a risk of food poisoning.

LEVI AND MARY MILLER, JUNCTION CITY, OH

- For food poisoning, drink water with a tablespoon of medicinal charcoal mixed in.

MRS. JOSEP MILLER, NAVARRE, OH

Diarrhea Relief

For diarrhea, take either charcoal or apple cider as capsules or in water. Take as soon as you feel stomach pain or suspect food poisoning.

MIRIAM BYLER, SPARTANSBURG, PA

BLOOD CLOTS

For blood clots, use nattokinase instead of a blood thinner 1 to 3 times a day for prevention. You can take as much as 15 to 50 mg a day when you have a blood clot.

MRS. HENRY A. SWARTZENTRUBER, LIBERTY, KY

CHEMO RELIEF

If you are taking chemo treatment for cancer, make tea out of basil leaves (or you can just eat the leaves). Good for nausea.

DAVID AND LAURA BYLER, NEW CASTLE, PA

REMEDY FOR TIREDNESS

Mix 1 tablespoon apple cider vinegar and 1 tablespoon honey in a glass of water. Take upon rising in the morning and before every meal. This is good for aches and pains and many other things.

DAVID AND LAURA BYLER, NEW CASTLE, PA

VARICOSE VEIN SALVE

1 pound lard
2 heaping handfuls marigold flower heads and leaves, chopped up

Heat lard until it crackles. Remove from heat and add chopped-up marigolds. Do not boil. Stir well. Cover and let stand overnight. Heat again and put through strainer or old cloth. Pour into jars and store in a cool place. Put on legs as needed.

ANNIE PEACHEY, LETART, WV

Prayer is not a way of getting what we want, but the way to become what God wants us to be.

INFLAMMATION

Heat 1 teaspoon turmeric in 1 cup of water. When cool enough, stir and drink. This fights all inflammation. Can also be used as a gargle for sore throat.

MRS. HENRY A. SWARTZENTRUBER, LIBERTY, KY

LACTOSE ISSUES?

Can't tolerate cow's milk? Set fresh milk in ice water for 12 hours, then skim off cream. Refrigerate cream for another 12 hours and separate cream again. Then take cream that was skimmed and add water to desired consistency. This can often be used for babies too. Removing whey makes milk more digestible.

K. HERTZLER, WEST SALISBURY, PA

HOMEMADE LAXATIVE

1 pint hot water
2 tablespoons Epsom salt
½ tablespoon cream of tartar

Combine and drink ½ cup or more first thing in the morning. To be used only occasionally as the need arises.

MARY STUTZMAN, WEST SALEM, OH

KIDNEY HEALTH AID

To prevent kidney or bladder infections, take a probiotic regularly.

MRS. DAVID KURTZ, SMICKSBURG, PA

URINARY TRACT INFECTION

For urinary tract infections, try apple cider vinegar pills or cranberry extract pills. Or drink apple cider vinegar in water. Do this every couple of hours and drink plenty of water. For maintenance, do this once or twice a day. Cranberry extract pills work better than a regular cranberry pill. They will also be darker in color.

MIRIAM BYLER, SPARTANSBURG, PA

MOOD LIFTER

For a mood lifter, try omegas like flaxseed a couple times a day. I think it helps so that I don't get so snappy with my children.

MIRIAM BYLER, SPARTANSBURG, PA

WEIGHT LOSS

Apple cider vinegar is helpful in melting excess pounds. Simply drink a glass of warm water with a single teaspoon of vinegar stirred in before each meal. It moderates the over-robust appetite and melts away fat.

MIRIAM BRENNEMAN, MORLEY, MI

Flaxseed for Prostate

Flaxseed is said to help slow the growth of prostate tumors.

DAVID AND LAURA BYLER, NEW CASTLE, PA

Grape Juice Diet

Eat not a bite during the forenoon. At 7:00 a.m., start slowly sipping on a 24-ounce bottle of unsweetened grape juice. Finish the bottle by 10:00 a.m. Wait until noon to eat lunch, avoiding pork and processed foods. Eat supper as usual.

Doing this each morning for 6 weeks usually wipes the body of cancer and many ailments. Prostate and bone cancer require more time.

For a child or small person, a 12-ounce bottle of unsweetened grape juice is enough.

If your stomach is weak or affected by the juice, start over the next day using smaller amounts of juice or add half water. Gradually increase juice. Shortly the stomach will be strengthened enough to take all the juice without water.

SADIE BYLER, FRAZEYSBURG, OH

Wisdom has two parts: having much to say and not saying much at all.

CARPAL TUNNEL SYNDROME

Some surgeries may be prevented by taking vitamin B6 and doing some exercises. Press bottom of chin with both thumbs for several minutes at least once daily. Also, press the tip of your pinkie finger and thumb together, then, resisting, try to pull them apart with your other hand. This builds up wrist muscles.

BARBARA E. YODER, GILMAN, WI

HAIR LOSS

Take Bio-B 100 (vitamin B complex from a health food store). Also, make tea of sage leaves in 1 pint hot water. Add 1 tablespoon boric acid. Massage tea into scalp daily.

BARBARA E. YODER, GILMAN, WI

ITCHY SCALP REMEDY

Wash hair with shampoo free of sodium lauryl sulphate, rinse, and then cover whole scalp with pure apple cider vinegar and let sit for 3 to 5 minutes. Rinse again.

MRS. KRISTINA BYLER, CRAB ORCHARD, KY

HEAD LICE

- For head lice, use just plain Shaklee Basic H. Put Basic H on the head the first week and do not wash the head until the end of the week. Do that until the lice are gone. The hair will get a little greasy, but it works. I put Basic H on the head Monday and Tuesday or skip Tuesday and put it on Wednesday.

MRS. HENRY A. SWARTZENTRUBER, LIBERTY, KY

- If you think you might have or get lice, wash your hair with a couple drops of kerosene in the water.

MIRIAM BYLER, SPARTANSBURG, PA

Nothing is as strong as gentleness or as gentle as real strength.

BATH AND BODY TIPS

HOT BATH SOAK

When the day has been long and trying and you are overtired, a hot bath will be wonderful relief. Add 1 cup Epsom salt and 2 tablespoons dry mustard. Your aching muscles will feel renewed the next morning.

Add baking soda to bathwater to kill perspiration odor.

LIZZIE H. STUTZMAN, GILMAN, WI

LAVENDER BATH SPA SALTS

2 cups Epsom salt
½ cup baking soda
10 to 15 drops lavender essential oil
Purple food coloring

Combine salt, soda, and oil in a stainless steel bowl, rubbing together with hands until very well combined. Add food coloring to create desired shade of lavender. Package in small clear cellophane bags and tie with ribbons. To use: Add desired amount to your bathwater and dissolve.

Variations:

- Use rose essential oil and tint the bath salts pink.
- Use jasmine essential oil and tint the bath salts yellow.
- Use eucalyptus essential oil and tint the bath salts pale green.

KATHRYN TROYER, RUTHERFORD, TN

Vanilla-Lavender Bath Salts

2 cups Epsom salt
½ cup baking soda
¼ cup sea salt (optional)
10 drops vanilla essential oil or
    1 teaspoon vanilla extract

10 drops lavender essential oil
A few drops food
    coloring (optional)

Place all ingredients in mixing bowl and mix until well blended. Store in airtight container for up to 6 months. When ready to use, pour ¼ cup bath salts into warm bathwater. Relax and enjoy the calming scents.

Try replacing lavender and vanilla essential oils with oil blends of your choice.

Benefits of salt baths include stress relief, reduced muscle and joint aches, improved circulation, headache relief, improved sleep, improved skin hydration, and help for acne, eczema, or other skin problems.

ADA J. MAST, KALONA, IA

Dry Skin Soak

1 cup baking soda
2 cups Epsom salt
1 drop peppermint essential oil
2 drops bergamot or orange essential oil

Add all ingredients to bathtub full of hot water. Soak and relax for 20 to 30 minutes.

EMMA MILLER, BALTIC, OH

Lavender Water

Fill the top of your steamer juicer with lavender flowers, stems, and leaves. Add 2 pints or less of water to the bottom part. Cover and set on stove on very low heat. Let steam for a couple of days or until there is no more color in the lavender. Add as much glycerin to the water to equal the water that remains. It smells like lavender oil. Have fun using it as you wish.

MALINDA M. GINGERICH, SPARTANSBURG, PA

Cracked Heels

Liquid bandage works wonders for dry, cracked heels.

NATHAN AND ANNA FISHER, SALISBURY, PA

Body Odor

For body odor, bad breath, and the like, try taking liquid chlorophyll.

MIRIAM BYLER, SPARTANSBURG, PA

*Worry is interest paid on
trouble before it is due.*

Deodorant

¼ cup organic coconut oil
1 tablespoon beeswax
¼ cup baking soda
¼ cup cornstarch

1 tablespoon arrowroot powder
6 drops essential oil of choice
8 drops tea tree oil

Put some water in saucepan. Put coconut oil and beeswax in canning jar and place in saucepan of water. Heat water to melt oil over low heat. Add baking soda, cornstarch, arrowroot powder, essential oil, and tea tree oil to jar and mix well. Pour mixture into little jars and let sit for several hours to solidify. Apply with fingertips.

SADIE BYLER, FRAZEYSBURG, OH

Homemade Toothpaste

Mix equal amounts of baking soda and table salt. Use to brush teeth.

SUSAN SCHWARTZ, BERNE, IN

Tooth Powder

2 parts baking soda
1 part sea salt
1 part cream of tartar

Mix baking soda, salt, and cream of tartar; then add any of the following essential oil(s) to your preferred strength:
Peppermint: Kills germs and freshens breath
Clove: Kills germs and fights infection
Thieves: Reduces plaque (use small amount)
Basil: Reduces plaque (use small amount)

MALINDA M. GINGERICH, SPARTANSBURG, PA

Homemade Clay Toothpaste

¾ cup Redmond bentonite clay
2 teaspoons Himalayan salt
2 teaspoons baking soda
4 teaspoons xylitol sweetener
2 drops peppermint oil

2 teaspoons black walnut
  powder (optional)
½ cup water (more or
  less, depending on
  desired consistency)

Mix all ingredients well and store in an airtight container.

KATIE FISHER, AARONSBURG, PA

Beeswax Lip Balm

¼ cup grated beeswax
3 tablespoons coconut oil

2 tablespoons cocoa butter
1 tablespoon almond oil

Mix ingredients together and heat gently in a double boiler until everything is melted. Pour into small tins or lip balm tubes.

MaryAnn Kempf, Winterset, IA

Honey Face Wash

⅓ cup unscented liquid
   Castile soap
⅓ cup raw honey
3 tablespoons distilled water

2 tablespoons sweet almond
   oil or olive oil
2 tablespoons aloe vera gel
20 to 40 drops essential oils

Mix all together. Shake a little before each use. Put in a foaming hand soap dispenser. Massage a small amount on your face. Rinse with lukewarm water. It tightens your skin.

Mary Ann Byler, New Wilmington, PA

No one has ever choked to death by swallowing her pride.

Shampoo

Flake 1 bar castile soap. In saucepan, melt soap in 1 pint boiling water, then cool. Put soap mixture in bowl and add 1 egg. Beat with beater. Pour in jar. After it has settled, it is ready to use. This shampoo will keep fine on the bathroom shelf.

TOBY AND RACHEL HERTZLER, CHARLOTTE COURT HOUSE, VA

Hair Rinse

- Put vinegar in rinse water to rinse your hair to prevent tangles. Use ¼ to ½ cup.

MIRIAM BYLER, SPARTANSBURG, PA

- Use a few tablespoons vinegar and 1 tablespoon baking soda in water for rinsing your hair.

MRS. LEVI J. STUTZMAN, WEST SALEM, OH

Hair Tamer

Use cold-pressed extra-virgin coconut oil for more manageable hair. Rub a little on scalp and hair after it is washed and leave in.

LIZZIE CHRISTNER, BERNE, IN

Natural Hairspray

2 cups boiling water
8 teaspoons sugar
8 tablespoons rubbing alcohol
20 drops essential oil (optional)

Blend water and sugar until dissolved. Add alcohol and essential oil. Pour in a spray bottle. Spritz on hair as needed.

RUTHIE MILLER, LOUDONVILLE, OH

Hand Sanitizer

¾ cup rubbing alcohol
¼ cup aloe vera gel
10 drops lavender oil or lemon oil

Mix all ingredients and put in soap dispenser clearly marked as hand sanitizer.

ESTHER MILLER, FREDERICKTOWN, OH

Life is like a
roll of toilet paper.
The closer it gets to the
end, the faster it goes!

DAVID AND LAURA BYLER,
NEW CASTLE, PA

Foaming Hand Soap

⅔ cup unscented liquid castile soap
1⅓ cups distilled water
⅛ teaspoon essential oil of choice

Pour ingredients into empty foaming soap dispenser. Shake well. We like to use Three Thieves essential oil in this.

LINDA BURKHOLDER, FRESNO, OH

Basic Hand Soap

3 cups olive oil
3 cups coconut oil
2½ pounds lard or tallow
1 quart warm water

12½ ounces lye
4 ounces essential oil of choice
Chopped herbs (like
  spearmint) (optional)

In stockpot heat olive oil, coconut oil, and lard to melt. Cool to 90 to 96 degrees. In bowl slowly mix warm water with lye. Cool to 86 to 90 degrees. Mix lye into oils and stir with a straight spoon for a few minutes. Then stir occasionally until it traces (thickens enough that you could write your name on it). Add essential oil and optional herb. Mix well and pour into molds or trays. Cut while still a little soft. Let sit in molds or trays for 2 days; then separate into bars and let air-dry for 2 to 4 weeks.

MRS. JONAS GINGERICH, DALTON, OH

Homemade Hand Soap

3 tablespoons unscented
  castile soap
¾ teaspoon fractionated
  coconut oil

16 drops essential oil like Thieves,
  or 8 drops lavender or lemon

Put ingredients in an empty 8-ounce foaming soap dispenser and add water.

MRS. REUBEN (ANNA) LAPP, ROCKVILLE, IN

Soap Scraps

- When a bar of soap gets too small to use, there's no need to throw it away. Just break the scraps into small pieces and put them into an empty squeeze bottle. Fill the bottle with warm water and let it sit for at least a day. Now you have liquid soap.

RUTH BYLER, QUAKER CITY, OH

- Save scraps of soap and put into a square of flannel. Tie up the flannel and dip into boiling water. When the soap is soft, dip into cold water and shape soap into a tight ball. When soap hardens, remove from flannel. Use like you would a bar of soap.

Hand Cream

A good hand cream for cracked or chapped hands is equal amounts of coconut oil, shea butter, olive oil, and beeswax with 1 teaspoon vitamin E oil. Essential oil can be added. Lavender oil is a good addition. Adjust it as you wish. If you want it thinner, add more olive oil.

MRS. HENRY A. SWARTZENTRUBER, LIBERTY, KY

Baby Lotion

Instead of buying baby lotion, use pure olive oil on the baby. Olive oil makes baby's skin just as soft. If you use too much, it will feel greasy. A good way to do it is to put some olive oil in your hand, rub your hands together, and then massage the baby. It is relaxing and healthy.

MRS. HENRY A. SWARTZENTRUBER, LIBERTY, KY

Homemade Baby Wipes

1 roll heavy paper towels
1 cup water

2 capfuls rubbing alcohol
1 teaspoon baby wash

Cut paper towels in half. Fold up and put in container. Combine water, alcohol, and baby wash. Pour over towels. Put on lid and turn upside down until towels absorb liquid.

CLARA A. YODER, SUGAR GROVE, PA

Seeing ourselves as others see us will not do us much good, for we will not believe what we see.

You must forgive someone their faults or you will never get close enough to admire their goodness.

GARDENING TIPS

*He causeth the grass to grow for the cattle,
and herb for the service of man: that he
may bring forth food out of the earth.*

PSALM 104:14

Gardening

Plant and tend a garden—whether big or small. Gardening slows you down, relaxes you, and makes you appreciate the cycle of life.

Encourage Young Gardeners

If you have young children, be enthusiastic about teaching gardening. Some children will naturally have more interest in growing plants. Buy what you need to encourage their help—small wheelbarrow, watering cans, extra trowels, and so forth. And if you buy plants at the greenhouse, buy extra packs because inevitably little feet will accidentally trample some. Show the children how to plant the plants, but don't be too picky with the end results of their efforts.

Salome Beiler, Woodward, PA

Bright Tools

Paint garden tool handles a bright red or yellow to help you find them among the vegetation.

Salomie E. Glick, Howard, PA

Composting

You can use cardboard boxes, newspapers, leaves, manure, bark, coffee grounds, tea bags, eggshells, fruit and vegetable trimmings, grass clippings, and vines and stalks from the garden for compost. Turn the pile every now and then to hasten decomposition. When it turns black and fluffy and smells like earth, use it in your garden and flower beds to boost the soil and mulch. Start a new pile every once in a while.

Miriam Byler, Spartansburg, PA
Mrs. Chester Miller, Centerville, PA

One who works in a garden works hand in hand with God

PLANTING TIPS

SAVING SEEDS

- Peas: To save peas for seeds, do not pick a small portion of your peas. Once peas have dried on the plants, you can pick and shell them, having seeds for next year. You can do the same for green beans and peppers.

- Tomatoes: I take a nice tomato I'm slicing to eat and remove the seeds. I place them on a paper towel and let them dry there. When ready to plant, I pick them off the towel and stick them in the dirt.

- Watermelon and cantaloupe: I remove seeds from the melon we are going to eat and spread them on a paper towel to dry. When fully dried, I store them in small, marked bottles. I do the same for cucumbers.

MRS. JOSEPH MILLER, NAVARRE, OH

SIMPLE WAY TO SAVE AND START TOMATOES

Select a beautiful, large, healthy tomato. Cut a slice (or however many you want) out of the middle of the tomato. Fill a pot with garden dirt. Put the tomato slice on top. Put in storage (preferably in a cellar or cold storage area). Forget about it until spring. In February or March, bring the pot to a sunny location; add dirt on top of pot to cover seeds. Water and watch your tomatoes start to sprout. Once they are 2 inches tall, transplant to individual pots. Simple and fun!

It is best to use heirloom tomatoes. My great aunt, 91 years young, still does this as she has for years.

BARBIE ESH, PARADISE, PA

Egg Pots

Save egg cartons. Put half of an eggshell in each hole and fill with potting soil. Plant seeds in each one. When seeds sprout, transplant the entire eggshell to the garden. There will be less transplanting shock when you do this.

MALINDA M. GINGERICH, SPARTANSBURG, PA

April Is for Planting

April in the Midwest is a good time for planting roses, perennial flowers, and herbs. You can also direct seed carrots, greens, beets, and other root vegetables.

DAVID AND LAURA BYLER, NEW CASTLE, PA

Plant by the Moon

- Plant all root crops in the dark of the moon from full moon to new moon.

EMMA KURTZ, SMICKSBURG, PA

- If you plant and harvest red beets in the dark of the moon, they will keep their dark color.

MRS. JOSEP MILLER, NAVARRE, OH

Planting Carrots

- To get big carrots, use a place in the garden that was covered with leaves or hay in the fall. Rake away the debris and mound up a row. The secret to growing big carrots is in planting them very, very thin so they have all the room they need to grow. Using a place that had been well covered during winter leads to almost weed-free carrots.

RACHEL MILLER, MILLERSBURG, OH

- When you plant carrot seeds, water them well and cover with cardboard to keep them wet. Do not let the cardboard dry out until the seeds have sprouted. If you do this, you should not have a problem growing nice carrots.

MALINDA M. GINGERICH, SPARTANSBURG, PA

Planting Green Beans

Scatter wood ashes over where you plant green beans. Usually they will come up sooner.

ESTHER L. MILLER, FREDERICKTOWN, OH

PLANTING PICKLES

- Plant your pickle/cucumber seeds on the first day of summer (June 21) for a fast- and good-growing crop. By then your early garden produce will be done, and you'll have space for the pickles.

  EMMA MILLER, BALTIC, OH

- Make a small frame for your pickles and cucumbers to climb up. They stay firm and last longer.

  SALOMIE E. GLICK, HOWARD, PA

PLANTING POTATOES

- Before planting, coat seed potatoes in sulfur and/or lime. Spray potato plants with Basic H (from Shaklee) diluted in water for better yields.

  MRS. RAYMOND KAUFFMAN, LA PLATA, MO

- Put Epsom salt on the rows with the potatoes as you plant them to prevent bugs.

  LORENE HELMUTH, JUNCTION CITY, WI

- Plant potatoes in the Midwest on June 10, and you won't have many issues with bugs.

  DAVID AND LAURA BYLER, NEW CASTLE, PA

- Plant potatoes in the evening after sunset for fewer problems with bugs.

  MRS. LEVI J. STUTZMAN, WEST SALEM, OH

- Plant potatoes very close together and you won't have to weed between the rows.

  JOHN LLOYD AND SUSAN YODER, NEWAYGO, MI

PLANTING RADISHES

- Put wood ashes on the ground where you plant radishes to keep your radishes from becoming wormy.

  MALINDA M. GINGERICH, SPARTANSBURG, PA

- When planting radishes, put coffee grounds or black pepper in with the seeds to keep worms away.

  MRS. FREEMAN YODER, MILLERSBURG, OH
  ANNA KING, NEW CASTLE, IN

PLANTING SQUASH

To combat squash bugs that seem to strike just as you think you might get a good crop, dip the seeds briefly into untreated kerosene before planting. It will also work for Chinese cabbage seeds.

  ALVIN AND KATIE HERTZLER, SALISBURY, PA

- Choose a healthy plant to start. Dig a deep hole and add 1 teaspoon dry cement and 1 teaspoon Epsom salt. Set plant so that only top branches are out of the hole. Water. Fill hole with dirt. You'll have lots of tomatoes.

  BARBARA BEECHY, MANAWA, WI

- When transplanting tomato plants into the garden, put 1 teaspoon Epsom salt in each hole to help them yield more and larger tomatoes. It gives them potassium and calcium.

  MENNO J. YODER FAMILY, BERLIN, PA

- To keep blight from tomatoes put 1 tablespoon Epsom salt in each hole before planting tomatoes.

  SALOMIE E. GLICK, HOWARD, PA

- Put crushed eggshells under tomato plants when you plant them. It fertilizes the tomatoes and helps against blossom rot.

  NORA MILLER, MILLERSBURG, OH
  AARON AND EMMA GINGERICH, BREMAN, OH
  MRS. DAN GINGERICH, MOUNT AYR, IA

- A simple tomato blight remedy is to put at least a tablespoon dried milk on the roots when planting and scatter some around on top of the dirt.

  MRS. JOSEP MILLER, NAVARRE, OH

- Plant a whole egg in the same hole as tomato plants. As the egg decays, it feeds the plant.

Eat an apple, save the core; plant the seed and raise some more.

Rhubarb

If you have rocky soil and nothing much grows there, try planting rhubarb, especially if on the north side of a building. Cover plants thickly with horse manure after last frost for a good crop in spring. Harvest in months without Rs (May, June, July, and August).

ESTHER L. MILLER, FREDERICKTOWN, OH

Flower Bulbs

When planting bulbs, make sure the bottom of the bulb is in firm contact with the bottom of the planting hole. If not, there will be an air pocket between the two, which will cause the bulb to rot.

MRS. JOSEPH SCHWARTZ, BERNE, IN

Geraniums

To keep geraniums from year to year, leave them in their pots and place them in a dark corner of the basement where they won't freeze. Don't water them, and eventually they will die back. In February or March, when they start to grow leaves, start watering them and put them near a sunny window. By early spring, they'll have leaves and new sprouts. They bloom later than those from the greenhouse, but they are worth keeping. I've also done the same with begonias, but I cut the plant down before bringing it inside.

Another method: Dig up geraniums in autumn just before the first hard frost. Shake off the dirt from the roots and place plants in a paper bag. Store in a cool, dry place. Replant in spring and watch them come back to life.

MALINDA M. GINGERICH, SPARTANSBURG, PA

Hot Caps

Instead of buying hot caps for your early plants, use lightweight, plastic, gallon milk jugs. Cut off the bottom and place the top over your early plants. Leave the cap off for venting. Push the jug well into the ground to keep the wind from blowing it away.

Glass jars can also be used as hot caps. Tie twine around the bottom of the jar. Light a match to it. As soon as the twine has burned and the jar is still hot, dip the bottom in cold water. The jar will break where the twine was. The sun will shine through the glass jars/jugs.

MALINDA M. GINGERICH, SPARTANSBURG, PA

Whistle and hoe, sing as you go; shorten the row by the songs you know.

Companion Planting

Borage

Plant borage in pots throughout your vegetable garden. You'll attract bees that can help bring you an earlier crop. Don't plant borage directly into the ground, though, as it can be invasive like mint. Check yard sales and flea markets for inexpensive borage plants. The borage flower is a nice blue.

DAVID AND LAURA BYLER, NEW CASTLE, PA

Basil and Tomatoes

Plant basil among tomatoes. Basil may ward off bugs and improve the flavor of the tomatoes.

Dill and Tomatoes

Plant a few sprigs of dill near your tomato plants to prevent tomato worms.

DAVID AND LAURA BYLER, NEW CASTLE, PA

Melons and Onions

When planting watermelon or any vining crops in the spring, try planting onion bulbs around them to help keep away squash bugs.

SADIE BYLER, FRAZEYSBURG, OH

Marigold Guardians

Plant marigolds around your cucumbers, squash, and melons. The marigolds help to keep the bugs away while brightening your garden.

SARAH W. HERSHBERGER, MCKENZIE, TN

Companion Herbs

Plant dill among cabbage to attract beneficial bugs that will help control the pests. Plant or mulch with mint around members of the cabbage (*brassica*) family to deter bugs. Chamomile, chives, oregano, rosemary, sage, and thyme are all beneficial to cabbage.

Fertilizing and Managing

Invest in High Yields

You've already invested in seeds and plants, so you should spend a little extra on fertilizer like Hyrbrix and expect a large yield. Hyrbrix is much cheaper in large bags, and what's left over can be saved for next season. I also like that Hyrbrix is applied once and that is usually enough, while other fertilizers call for multiple applications.

SALOME BEILER, WOODWARD, PA

Garden Growth Spray

1 cup ammonia
2 cups vinegar

2 gallons water

Mix all ingredients and spray on tomatoes, beans, and more once a month. The mixture helps the plant bear fruit.

MELVIN AND BARBARA SCHLABACH, DAYTON, PA

Garden Spray

1 gallon lukewarm water
2 tablespoons Spray-N-Grow
2 tablespoons Pyola

1 tablespoon liquid fertilizer
1 tablespoon 3 percent peroxide
2 tablespoons soap shield

Mix lukewarm water and Spray-N-Grow. Let sit 15 to 20 minutes. Add remaining ingredients. Mix well and spray every 2 weeks after the sun is down or on a cloudy day. Do not spray when sunny as it may burn plants. This spray is a plant food, pest control, and blight spray for all garden plants.

TOBY AND RACHEL HERTZLER, CHARLOTTE COURT HOUSE, VA

Plant Boosters

- A tablespoon of castor oil followed by water brings sick plants out of a slump.

  Ruth Byler, Quaker City, OH

- Sprinkle Epsom salt on your garden plants just before a rain for beautiful plants and more bountiful harvest.

  Ida Byler, Frazeysburg, OH

Plant Food

1 teaspoon baking powder	½ teaspoon ammonia
1 teaspoon Epsom salt	1 gallon water
1 teaspoon saltpeter	

Stir all ingredients together. Water plant every 5 to 6 days with solution. Try it on your lazy African violets and watch them grow in volume and beauty. Works on vegetable plants too.

Mrs. Monroe Miller, Blanchard, MI
Emma Byler, New Wilmington, PA

Flower Booster

½ gallon hot water	1 tablespoon ammonia
1 tablespoon Epsom salt	1 tablespoon saltpeter
1 tablespoon baking powder	½ gallon cold water

Mix hot water, Epsom salt, baking powder, ammonia, and saltpeter until dissolved. Add cold water. Spray flowers every month. May also use on vegetable plants, tomatoes, peppers, melons, and more.

Melvin and Barbara Schlabach, Dayton, PA

Salt Asparagus

Sprinkle salt over your asparagus patch. Asparagus likes salt, and salt kills the weeds.

Emma Kurtz, Smicksburg, PA
Mrs. Josep Miller, Navarre, OH

Lettuce

For healthier, tastier lettuce, sprinkle some blood meal in the rows where the seeds are planted.

Mary E. Miller, Middlebury, IN

Pea Plants

For yellow-looking pea plants and to increase yield, sprinkle plain white sugar over the plants. Best to do just before a rain or to water them a little afterward.

Emma Kurtz, Smicksburg, PA

BLUEBERRY MULCH

Mulch blueberry plants with pine needles.

JOANN MILLER, FREDERICKTOWN, OH

GRAPES

- Apply approximately 1 cup regular table salt to mature, well-established grapevines in the spring.
- Use 1 gallon white vinegar and divide it among two grapevines, starting when they show buds until harvest, applying once a month. This helps fight black rot.

SADIE BYLER, FRAZEYSBURG, OH

SPRING GRAPE TREATMENT

2 cups sulfur
2 cups lime
4 pounds wood ash
1 cup salt
Mothballs

In early spring, dig around grapevines. Form a round ditch around the stalk, 6 inches from the stalk. Mix sulfur, lime, ash, and salt. Add enough water to make 1 gallon. Paint the thick part of the stalk. Pour the rest on the stalk and over the roots so that the dirt catches it. Make bundles of mothballs and hang here and there on the vines to keep bugs away.

Later in spring, about when little grapes form, put 1 gallon homemade vinegar to each stalk. Mulch them with plenty of manure, and if a dry year, water every so often.

TOBY AND RACHEL HERTZLER, CHARLOTTE COURT HOUSE, VA

GRAPE FERTILIZER 1

1 tablespoon baking soda
1 tablespoon Epsom salt
1 tablespoon vinegar
1 quart water

Mix and apply weekly to each grapevine. In April I also give each vine 1 pound Epsom salt dissolved in warm water. Then later that same week, I apply 1 gallon water with 2 tablespoons fish fertilizer.

JOHN K. BEILER JR., RONKS, PA

GRAPE FERTILIZER 2

1 cup apple cider vinegar
1 cup Epsom salt
1 cup baking soda
1 gallon water

Mix and give to grapevine. One recipe feeds one vine. Feed every month of the year, except for when the ground is frozen.

MELVIN AND BARBARA SCHLABACH, DAYTON, PA

Grapes and Raspberries

1 gallon wood ash
1 gallon white lime
1 handful sulfur powder
1 handful Epsom salt

Mix well and apply a large handful of mixture around each grape and berry plant in February, March, and April. Apply again in the fall.

Sadie Byler, Frazeysburg, OH

Healthy Berry and Grapevine Spray

2 cups Epsom salt
1 gallon hot water
1 tablespoon captan (if available)
or 2 tablespoons Sevin powder
1 tablespoon fish emulsion

Dissolve Epsom salt in hot water, stirring well. Add remaining ingredients, mix well. Spray on raspberry plants, strawberry plants, grapevines, and fruit trees. This should be used 2 or 3 times in spring. Once a month is best through March, April, and May.

S.H., PA

Mrs. John K. Beiler Jr., Ronks, PA

The highest reward for a person's toil is not what they get for it but what they become by it.

One today
is worth two
tomorrows.

Raspberry Fertilizer

1 gallon lime   2 handfuls sulfur
1 gallon wood ash

Mix and apply 1 handful to each plant once a month in February, March, and April, and when the berries are starting to show. Use once again in the fall. Also good for grapes and fruit trees.

Mrs. Josep Miller, Navarre, OH
Mrs. Henry A. Swartzentruber, Liberty, KY

Rhododendron

Does your rhododendron have only sparse blooms? Make a citrus puree. Whenever you have grapefruit, oranges, or lemons, cut up the rinds and puree them in your blender. Pour this around the rhododendron in the winter and spring and the plant will be covered with blossoms. Works on azaleas too.

Ruth Byler, Quaker City, OH

Rhubarb

- For long, thick, juicy rhubarb stalks, cover the bed thickly with up to 1 foot of horse manure in the fall and leave on through the growing season. It will compost by summer. You can hardly put on too much manure.

Rebecca Herschberger, Bear Lake, MI

- In the fall, mulch rhubarb with 12 to 18 inches of old straw or dead leaves. Cover with an old bedsheet and weigh down with rocks or pieces of wood to keep it in place. Remove the sheet in spring when you see the crown is pushing through. Then mulch thickly with old manure.

Sadie Byler, Frazeysburg, OH

Roses

Feed your roses by working rotten banana skins into the soil near the base of your rosebushes. The potassium in the skins gives them a power-packed boost. Blend the bananas skins to make it easy to mix them into the dirt. Dig a deep hole for roses. Pour the blender full of banana skins into the hole. Cover with 2 to 3 inches of dirt. Plant roses on top as usual.

Toby and Rachel Hertzler, Charlotte Court House, VA
Malinda M. Gingerich, Spartansburg, PA

Strawberry Booster

Give your extra milk to your strawberry plants during times when they're not bearing fruit. Pour some on each plant when the sun is shining. Milk will produce a heavy yield the next season and berries will not be seedy.

EMMA KURTZ, SMICKSBURG, PA

Milk Fortifier

Whenever you have extra or sour milk, dilute it with water and pour it on your vegetable plants. It is also good for raspberry plants.

MARTHA MILLER, EDGAR, WI

Rotting Pepper Remedy

1½ tablespoons 35 percent peroxide (food grade)	1 tablespoon sugar
	1 gallon water

Mix all ingredients and spray the plant with mixture. It stopped the rotting right away for me. Also good to use on strawberry plants.

WOLLIE SCHLABACH, SMICKSBURG, PA

Peppers and Tomatoes Booster

Grow your peppers and tomatoes bigger and tastier by using eggshells. Soak crushed eggshells in water for 24 hours. Use the water on your plants to energize them.

ESTHER MILLER, ROSSITER, PA

Tomato Blight Remedy

1 gallon water	1 tablespoon baking soda
1 tablespoon saltpeter	1 teaspoon ammonia
1 tablespoon Epsom salt	

Mix ingredients well and give 1 pint to each plant every 2 weeks. Don't water them when the sun shines. Also good for melons and more.

SCHWARTZ FAMILY, SALEM, IN

REBECCA HERSCHBERGER, BEAR LAKE, MI

Tomato Blight

Mix 1 tablespoon bleach to 1 gallon water and spray on tomato plants twice a week for blight.

MALINDA M. GINGERICH, SPARTANSBURG, PA

Pruning and Tying Tomatoes

For big, beautiful tomatoes, trim off the suckers or shoots every 2 to 3 weeks during the growing season. Then pound in stakes and tie up the plants at intervals. They will not rot as easily when they are off the ground.

REBECCA HERSCHBERGER, BEAR LAKE, MI

MALINDA M. GINGERICH, SPARTANSBURG, PA

The bridges you cross before you come to them are over rivers that aren't there.

When someone slings mud at you, let it dry and it will fall off.

TRIM TO GROW

To grow bushy flowers (like petunia, impatiens, etc.), trim off all flowers when transplanting.

MRS. MONROE MILLER, BLANCHARD, MI
DAVID AND LAURA BYLER, NEW CASTLE, PA

THINNING TREE FRUIT

In June spray small fruit hanging on limbs with a mixture of 6 ounces liquid Sevin to 1 gallon water. The weak fruit will dry up and drop off.

MRS. REUBEN N. BYLER, DAYTON, PA

VEGETABLE BLIGHT

Cook 1 small bar Ivory soap in 1 quart water until melted. Add 4 ounces Borax, 4 ounces saltpeter, and 1 pint washing ammonia. This will turn into a hard jelly. To use, add 1 cup mixture to hot water in a bucket and stir to dissolve. Fill bucket with cold water and mix. Spray on vegetables with a sprayer or sprinkling can to rid blight on tomatoes, celery, and more.

MRS. LEVI J. STUTZMAN, WEST SALEM, OH

POWDERY MILDEW

1 teaspoon vinegar   3 to 4 drops soap
1 teaspoon Listerine

Mix in a spray bottle and fill with water. Spray affected area.

EMMA BYLER, NEW WILMINGTON, PA

PLANT WILT

When your vegetable plants, including cabbage, lettuce, and more, wilt and rot, fungus could be the cause. Work lots of garden sulfur into the soil. It can burn the roots, so be sure to work it in very well. It should fix the problem.

TOBY AND RACHEL HERTZLER, CHARLOTTE COURT HOUSE, VA

WILT FIGHTER

To save wilting cucumber or melon vines, when you first notice the wilt, apply ½ cup ammonia in 1 gallon of water.

MELVIN AND BARBARA SCHLABACH, DAYTON, PA

REUSE DISHWATER

When you're done doing dishes, dump your water on your flowers. They love it.

IDA GIROD, SALEM, IN

PEST AND WEED CONTROL

NATURAL GARDEN PESTICIDE

Mix 1 tablespoon of Shaklee Basic H into 1 gallon water. Spray all vegetable plants except tomatoes. Spray every 10 days, more if needed.

MRS. LEVI J. STUTZMAN, WEST SALEM, OH

PLANT INSECTICIDAL SOAP

Make your own insecticidal soap for pennies. Mix ¾ teaspoon Murphy's oil soap into 1 quart warm water. Spray on your garden and houseplants.

DAVID AND LAURA BYLER, NEW CASTLE, PA

SAFE INSECT SPRAY FOR GARDENS

1 teaspoon red pepper	1 teaspoon onion salt
1 teaspoon garlic salt	1 pint hot water

Mix all ingredients and let stand 2 days. Strain. Put in gallon sprayer and fill with water.

JERRY AND MARY GIROD, CARLISLE, KY

LIME

Hydrated lime—what you buy at the feed mill—is good to use as a garden dust. Dust any vegetable plant with it to help reduce bugs. It is also good to dust potatoes before planting. Rhubarb plants also like lime.

MRS. LEVI J. STUTZMAN, WEST SALEM, OH
LACY GLICK, MILL HALL, PA

BONE MEAL

Bone meal works well when spread by hand around berry patches. It keeps away bugs while feeding the plants.

VERA MAST, KALONA, IA

MOTHBALL DEFENDERS

Scatter mothballs by hand on the ground around trees to prevent worms in fruit. May also help prevent blight on scrubs and vines.

VERA MAST, KALONA, IA

SALT

Try sprinkling salt on your cabbage, cauliflower, and broccoli transplants to keep worms away.

TOBY AND RACHEL HERTZLER, CHARLOTTE COURT HOUSE, VA

SUGAR TONIC

To kill bugs and worms in the garden, sprinkle plants with water, then sprinkle with white sugar.

VIOLA BEECHY, MANAWA, WI

WOOD ASH

I use wood ashes to dust my garden plants and spread around the house to keep away bugs. I also coat radish seeds in ash before planting to help with worms. Old advice is to put enough wood ashes around rhubarb to keep weeds away.

MRS. LEVI J. STUTZMAN, WEST SALEM, OH

Disappointments are like weeds in the garden; you can let them grow and take over your life, or you can rout them out and let the flowers sprout.

One thorn of experience is worth more than a wilderness of advice or warning.

Reflectors

In the garden, hang old CD disks, aluminum pie pans, or reflective tape on fence posts, trellises, and the like to scare aware birds and other pests.

June Bugs

Adding lime to your garden and yard will discourage june bugs from laying their eggs.

CHRISTINA PEIGHT, BELLEVILLE, PA

Cabbage Saver

1 cup flour   1 tablespoon sugar
1 teaspoon red pepper

Mix all ingredients together. Dust it over cabbage and similar garden plants. Repeat about once a week, or sooner if rain washes it off.

MELVIN AND BARBARA SCHLABACH, DAYTON, PA
MRS. FREEMAN YODER, MILLERSBURG, OH

Aphid Remedy

For aphids on vegetable plants, spray with a strong solution of Ivory dish soap mixed in water.

SARAH W. HERSHBERGER, McKENZIE, TN

Cucumber Beetle Control

1 tablespoon ammonia   1 teaspoon baking soda
1 teaspoon Epsom salt   1 gallon water
1 tablespoon saltpeter

Combine ingredients and pour around roots of cucumber vines. Drench roots every 2 weeks. Makes enough for 6 plants.

TOBY AND RACHEL HERTZLER, CHARLOTTE COURT HOUSE, VA

Buggy Beans

To keep bugs off beans, mix 2 cups sorghum molasses with 1 gallon water and spray until leaves are wet. Repeat after each rain.

MRS. RAYMOND KAUFFMAN, LA PLATA, MO

Potato Bug Spray

¼ cup peroxide   1 gallon water
¼ cup Shaklee Basic H

Mix ingredients and spray on potato plants when the sun is not shining. If this isn't strong enough, increase the peroxide and Basic H to ½ cup each to 1 gallon water.

MELVIN AND BARBARA SCHLABACH, DAYTON, PA

Fruit Tree Spray

Combine 1 gallon water and 4 ounces ground ginger and bring to the boiling point. Use as a general bug spray on fruit trees.

MRS. REUBEN N. BYLER, DAYTON, PA

Fruit Tree Bug Traps

Combine water, apple cider vinegar, and sugar. Pour into a heavy plastic jug with a handle loop to tie twine around. Fill only about ¼ full, and add a banana peel to each jug. Hang in the middle of the tree as best you can reach. Refresh the contents when it fills with bugs. Large trees may require more than one jug.

Raspberries

Try to keep ahead of those little worms in red raspberries by picking berries daily, even if they are only light red. They'll redden up a day after picked.

REBECCA HOCHSTETLER, CENTERVILLE, MI

For Bugs on Roses

1 teaspoon Ivory dish soap
1 tablespoon baking soda
1 gallon water

Mix and spray on plants.

KATIE ZOOK, APPLE CREEK, OH

When the outlook is not good, try the up look.

Moles

- For moles in your yard, punch holes in runways with a small stick and pour a little kerosene in and cover tightly to shut the light out. They disappear immediately.

  MIRIAM BRENNEMAN, MORLEY, MI

- If your garden is infested with moles, planting garlic or leeks will make them leave.

  LACY GLICK, MILL HALL, PA

Rabbits

Are rabbits eating your lettuce? Dust it with talcum powder and they'll leave it alone.

MALINDA M. GINGERICH, SPARTANSBURG, PA
RUBY MILLER, AUBURN, KY

Raccoons

To keep raccoons out of the garden, lay loosely crumpled newspaper throughout the patch. Anchor with rocks or dirt clods on corners. The "news" scares them, and they will not walk on it.

SADIE BYLER, FRAZEYSBURG, OH

Snails

Put crushed eggshells around lettuce and flowers to help keep snails away. Salt also kills snails, but it will also kill plants.

EMMA KURTZ, SMICKSBURG, PA

Reused Laundry Water

When you are done doing laundry with lye soap, fill your sprinkling can with the water and water green beans, broccoli, cauliflower, and cabbage to keep bugs off. I do it twice a week, and it helps.

IDA GIROD, SALEM, IN

Mulching

- Don't let weeds take over your garden. Mulch in spring; then weekly weeding will not be a big job.

  SALOME BEILER, WOODWARD, PA

- Use old newspaper under mulch to keep down weeds. Mulch may be anything like grass clippings, old hay or straw, or dried leaves. I like to use aged (at least one year) horse manure mixed with sawdust bedding. Does a great job in flower beds.

  MRS. BETHANY MARTIN, HOMER CITY, PA

- After your plants are up, layer flattened cardboard boxes around your plants or in the rows and cover with mulch of straw, old hay, aged manure, compost, or the like. It really helps with controlling weeds and retaining moisture.

  ELIZABETH SHETLER, BRINKHAVEN, OH

- We like to mulch our garden once the plants are 4 to 5 inches tall. Grass clippings will pack down and eliminate the need for hoeing and, if thick enough, prevent most weeds. Harvesting produce is much more enjoyable and relaxing when you don't have to search through weeds to find the veggies.

  REBECCA HOCHSTETLER, CENTERVILLE, MI

- Bag your leaves in fall and store until next summer. Use them to mulch corn and other garden plants. We also pile lots of leaves around our blueberries. This keeps most of the weeds down and there's no need to mow around the plants.

  RACHEL MILLER, MILLERSBURG, OH

Fall Cover Crop

In the fall, as soon as the garden is empty, plant cover crop of oats and radish. Broadcast and cover with a light layer of straw for better soil and fewer bug problems. Plow under in spring.

LIZZIE CHRISTNER, BERNE, IN

*It is not where
we are but who
we are that creates
our happiness.*

Organic Weed Killer

1 gallon white or apple cider vinegar
1 cup table salt
1 tablespoon liquid dish soap

In a bucket or large kettle, mix vinegar and salt. Stir briskly until salt is dissolved. (You may also heat a quart of the vinegar and all the salt on the stove top, stirring briskly until the salt dissolves. Add remaining vinegar.) Add soap to the mixture and stir. Pour into a sprayer and spray unwanted vegetation. Wash out your sprayer thoroughly when finished. Note: Keep away from garden vegetables and flowers.

Mrs. Daniel Wickey, Berne, IN
Marie D. Hershberger, Laurelville, OH
Mrs. Reuben N. Byler, Dayton, PA

Natural Weed Killer

Small batch:	Large batch:
1 quart vinegar	1 gallon vinegar
1 cup dish soap	1 bottle dish soap
1 cup salt	3 cups salt
1 gallon water	4 to 5 gallons water

Mix all together and spray on weeds. Store what isn't used for later in well-marked container. Keep out of reach of children.

S.H., PA
Rebecca Herschberger, Bear Lake, MI

Weed Killer

1 gallon vinegar
2 cups Epsom salt
¼ cup Dawn dish soap
(original blue)

Mix and spray. It will kill anything you spray it on. Best applied in the morning after the dew has evaporated and on a warm and sunny day.

Mrs. Josep Miller, Navarre, OH

Poison Ivy

To remove poison ivy, mix together a gallon of soapy water and 3 pounds of salt. Spray area well.

Edith Mast, Bertha, MN

HARVESTING

Asparagus

- Cut all asparagus tops off beneath the ground, not above. When the stalk is cut, the stump bleeds and takes strength out of the roots. When loose dirt covers the stump, it can't bleed.

  MALINDA M. GINGERICH, SPARTANSBURG, PA

- Young, slender, firm stalks with closed, compact tips are the best. All the green parts should be tender and edible after cooking. The white parts should be cut away before cooking, but they may be saved for flavoring soups and stews. Asparagus is a fairly perishable vegetable. Once cut, it ages fast. Wilted asparagus has opened tips, which may be discolored, and tough, leathery stalks.

  KATHRYN DETWEILER, WEST FARMINGTON, OH

Broccoli and Cabbage

Once you cut off the first head of broccoli, leave the root part with the leaves in the ground. That will grow more broccoli throughout the summer. After you cut a head of cabbage, leave the leaves and root. You should be able to harvest 3 to 4 small heads later.

MRS. JOSEPH MILLER, NAVARRE, OH

Green Beans

If you have extra green beans in the garden, you can let them hang on the plants until they mature. Beans can then be shelled and used as soup beans.

MRS. BETHANY MARTIN, HOMER CITY, PA

Fresh-Cut Flowers

- Fresh-cut flowers will last longer in a vase if you add ¼ teaspoon (or 20 drops) of Clorox bleach to each quart of water.

REBECCA HERSCHBERGER, BEAR LAKE, MI
MRS. JOSEP MILLER, NAVARRE, OH

- To keep cut flowers fresh, put 2 tablespoons vinegar and 3 tablespoons sugar in a quart of water.

ANNA KING, NEW CASTLE, IN

Cut Flower Preservative

1 quart water
½ teaspoon Clorox bleach
1 teaspoon sugar
2 teaspoons lemon juice or white vinegar

Mix all and use to preserve cut flowers.

SADIE FISHER, AARONSBURG, PA

Dahlias

Never dig up your dahlia bulbs before November 15. Store them in a cool, dry place. If any of the bulbs are dead looking in spring, put them in a glass of water. Sometimes they will start to sprout and can be planted, though not always.

MRS. DANIEL WICKEY, BERNE, IN

You cannot hope to enjoy the harvest without laboring in the field.
DAVID AND LAURA BYLER, NEW CASTLE, PA

HOUSEPLANTS

WATERING HOUSEPLANTS

- Collect rainwater and give it to your houseplants. They will love it!

  MARY ELLEN MILLER, APPLE CREEK, OH

- Use the water from hard-boiled eggs to water your houseplants. It helps to feed them, and you won't have to buy other fertilizer. You can also soak eggshells in water for 2 weeks. They may get smelly, but the water also works great as a plant fertilizer.

  LOVINA D. GINGERICH, MOUNT AYR, IA

- Put 1 teaspoon ammonia in ½ gallon water to water your houseplants and help them brighten up.

  MALINDA M. GINGERICH, SPARTANSBURG, PA

HOUSEPLANT FERTILIZER

Place crushed eggshells in a gallon jar. Cover half full with boiling water. Let sit until cool, then finish filling the jar with cold water. Use this to fertilize houseplants. Leaves will turn a healthy dark green.

AARON AND EMMA GINGERICH, BREMAN, OH

MILK BATH

Diluted milk will keep mites off houseplants and outdoor plants.

VERA MAST, KALONA, IA

BOSTON FERNS

If fern leaves turn yellow, slice a raw potato and put it on top of the soil. This will draw out worms that are usually responsible for the issue.

CHRISTMAS CACTUS

Give Christmas cactus plants 1 teaspoon castor oil every week during the month of October if you want them to bloom for Christmas.

EDITH N. CHRISTNER, BERNE, IN

*It isn't your position
that makes you happy;
it's your disposition.*

LIVESTOCK AND WILDLIFE CARE TIPS

And God made the beast of the earth after his kind, and cattle after their kind, and every thing that creepeth upon the earth after his kind: and God saw that it was good.

GENESIS 1:25

MILK COW MASTITIS

When a cow has mastitis, mix equal parts vinegar and rubbing alcohol and rub on the cow's udder. We have had good results with it.

MRS. LEVI J. STUTZMAN, WEST SALEM, OH

PIG FEED

If you have a cow, dump your extra milk or whey from making cheese in the pig trough. Include any bad produce from the garden. Then you'll have healthy sausage when it comes time to butcher.

REBECCA HOCHSTETLER, CENTERVILLE, MI

SORGHUM MOLASSES

When sorghum molasses is too old for use in cooking and baking, drizzle it over the cows' and horses' feed. It's a good source of iron and minerals for them.

MRS. LEVI MILLER, JUNCTION CITY, OH

Our deeds speak so loudly that our words can't be heard.

Horse Spray

2 cups **Dawn dish soap**
2 cups **kerosene**
4 cups **white vinegar**
6 cups **water**

Put all ingredients in a plastic gallon jug and mix or shake together. To use fill a plastic spray bottle half full. My husband likes to spray this on the horse in summer before we leave home. Clearly mark the bottle and jug "Horse Spray" and store away from the reach of children.

S.H., PA

Deep Cuts on Horses

For a deep cut that keeps bleeding, put cayenne pepper on the cut and the bleeding will soon quit. Also helps the cut heal faster.

Susan Bontrager, Lagrange, IN

Simple Horse Liniment

We never buy horse liniment. Every time the horses have swollen legs or cuts, we put comfrey leaves in hot water. Let sit long enough to give water a good color. Then put on a cloth as hot as you can stand. Do 1 or 2 applications a day until the cut heals. When leaves are done soaking, put them against the wound and wrap them in place.

Sadie Byler, Reynoldsville, PA

Colic in Horses

Give 4 ounces of aromatic compound.

Mrs. Joseph Schwartz, Berne, IN

Nonlaying Hens

- If your hens don't start laying eggs but are old enough, start adding 1 tablespoon red pepper to 1 quart of layer mash. Add just enough warm water to make the mash wet. Give in the morning and again in the afternoon, and you should soon be getting eggs.

  Rachel Miller, Millersburg, OH

- In winter, offer warm water to hens first thing in the morning.

Chicken Dust

Put wood ashes in a tub for chickens to dust bathe in.

Mrs. Levi J. Stutzman, West Salem, OH

Eggshells

Crush dry eggshells and use as you would oyster shells to increase calcium in chicken feed.

Verna Gingerich, Mount Ayr, IA

Red Pepper

Sprinkle red pepper over chicken feed in winter to help generate warmth.

Verna Gingerich, Mount Ayr, IA

Chicken and Bird Feed

Save and dry melon seeds. Mix into your birdseed and your feathered friends will love you for it.

Lydia Miller, Loudonville, OH

Feathers Off Butchered Chickens

To singe tiny feathers off chicken carcasses, squirt some 91 percent rubbing alcohol into an old pie pan. Light it with a match and use the small fire to burn the "hair" off the chicken. It makes cleaning chicken a lot easier. Caution: Do not add more alcohol before the fire has completely gone out.

Levi and Mary Miller, Junction City, OH

Chicken and Turkey Cones

We use cones to put our chickens in to behead and bleed them before scalding and plucking them. For turkeys, we use an old milk can with the bottom cut off. Fasten it upside down to a post. A dehorner tool works very well to behead them.

Levi and Mary Miller, Junction City, OH

Bird Suet

1 cup lard	2 cups cornmeal
1 cup peanut butter	¼ cup sugar
1 cup flour	Sunflower seeds
2 cups oatmeal	

In a pan, melt lard and peanut butter and blend. Add flour, oatmeal, cornmeal, and sugar; mix well. Mix in sunflower seeds. Press mixture into a pan and let harden. Cut into squares that fit suet feeders.

MALINDA M. GINGERICH, SPARTANSBURG, PA

Suet for the Birds

1 cup lard	2 cups cornmeal
1 cup crunchy peanut butter	1 cup flour
2 cups quick oats	½ cup sugar

Melt lard and peanut butter. Then stir in the remaining ingredients. Let cool then put in mesh bags and hang for the birds.

MRS. MONROE MILLER, BLANCHARD, MI

Hummingbird Feed

In a saucepan, combine 1 cup sugar and 4 cups water. Gently boil until sugar dissolves. Cool. Warning: Never use honey as it is fatal to the birds. Food coloring is also not good for them.

FEENIE BEILER, DELTA, PA

The reason a dog has so many friends?
He wags his tail instead of his tongue.
DAVID AND LAURA BYLER, NEW CASTLE, PA

Bird Cakes

2 cups cornmeal	½ cup molasses
6 cups water	½ teaspoon baking powder
½ cup bacon drippings	1 teaspoon red pepper
1 cup flour	Nuts
1 rounded tablespoon sand	Raisins

Mix cornmeal with water and bring to a boil. Cool. Add remaining ingredients. Mix in enough additional water to bind mixture together; pour into small foil pie pans. Bake at 400 degrees until brown. Hang the pans in a tree and watch the birds flock to the treat. If you make too much, freeze it for later.

RUTH BYLER, QUAKER CITY, OH

Peanut Butter Treats

- Smear peanut butter or lard onto pine cones and coat with birdseed. Bread crumbs or stale food can also be used to roll the smeared pine cones in.

RUTH BYLER, QUAKER CITY, OH

- Take the cardboard interior of a toilet paper roll or a pine cone and smear peanut butter over it. Roll in birdseed to fully coat. Hang outside for a special treat for your feathered friends.

IDA BYLER, FRAZEYSBURG, OH

- Smear leftover church peanut butter or old peanut butter on a tree trunk. Watch the birds enjoy it.

MALINDA M. GINGERICH, SPARTANSBURG, PA

Bird Treat

Pour bacon grease over leftover toast or bread. Let harden; then put a string through the center and tie it to a tree branch for the birds.

MALINDA M. GINGERICH, SPARTANSBURG, PA

Jelly Feeder

Nail some plastic jar lids on a board and fill with jelly for orioles and catbirds.

MALINDA M. GINGERICH, SPARTANSBURG, PA

Purple Martin Houses

Line your martin houses on the inside with aluminum foil. It keeps sparrows and starlings away.

MALINDA M. GINGERICH, SPARTANSBURG, PA

Squirrel Feeder

Hammer some long nails on a board and push ears of dried corn onto the nails for squirrels and birds.

MALINDA M. GINGERICH, SPARTANSBURG, PA

*If you trust,
you don't worry;
if you worry,
you don't trust.*

The secret of success in conversation is to be able to disagree without being disagreeable.

CRAFTING TIPS

She seeketh wool, and flax, and worketh willingly with her hands.

PROVERBS 31:13

SEWING TIPS

THREADING A NEEDLE

- To make it easier to thread a needle, cut the thread at an angle instead of straight across.

  MRS. REUBEN (ANNA) LAPP, ROCKVILLE, IN

- To quickly thread a needle, place a piece of white paper under your needle to help you see what you are doing.

  SALOMIE E. GLICK, HOWARD, PA

- A touch of lip balm makes thread easier to push through the eye of a needle.

- Running thread through soap or candle wax helps prevent knots, tangles, and raveling.

EASE OF SEWING

Poke pins and needles in the wax of a candle to help them slide through fabric more easily.

THIMBLES

To keep a thimble on your finger, blow into it once or twice before putting it on. The moisture from your breath will help hold it on.

PIN CATCHER

Tape a large, flat magnet to your sewing table to collect pins while sewing.

Holder for Needles

Save your prescription medicine bottles and use them to hold pins, needles, broken needles and pins to be trashed, knitting point protectors, buttons, snaps, and more. Clean the bottles carefully, and remove the labels before repurposing them for your supplies.

Loose Buttons

For an emergency stop of an unraveling button, dab the center of the button with clear nail polish to hold the thread secure.

Double the Thread

When putting hooks and eyes or snaps on clothes, try doubling the thread before you put it through the needle. Saves you some time.

Mrs. Daniel Wickey, Berne, IN

Blood Drops

To remove bloodstains from needle or pin prinks, immediately use your own saliva or icy-cold water to dissolve it.

Soap Markers

When your bar soap is thin, dry it and keep it to mark patterns onto dark fabric when sewing. It marks easily and washes out.

Miriam Byler, Spartansburg, PA
Miriam Brenneman, Morley, MI
Lizzie Christner, Berne, IN

Lost Pins

A magnet attached to a long handle helps pick up pins from the floor.

Reused Elastic

When shorts wear out, the elastic often is not worn out. Cut it off and reuse it. You can cut halfway through lengthwise. It frays, but if you use it inside seams, it won't keep fraying.

Miriam Byler, Spartansburg, PA

Sewing Machine Oil

After oiling the sewing machine, sew through a scrap of fabric to help distribute the oil and also to catch any excess before you sew good fabric.

Crib Sheets

You can make your own crib sheets. Cut fabric (even an old sheet) to 42 x 64 inches. Cut a 6-inch square out of each of the 4 corners. Sew corners together. Turn a seam around the outer edge, adding narrow elastic to the short (bottom) end.

Miriam Byler, Spartansburg, PA

A Plan for Fabric Scraps

When you cut out clothes to sew and have scraps left over that are too small for another garment, cut out comforter/quilt blocks in 3-, 4-, or 6-inch squares (whatever size you can get out of them). Doing this immediately with scraps will keep your scrap drawer from getting messy. Store blocks in one place; then when you have enough squares and some extra time, sew them together.

Rebecca Hochstetler, Centerville, MI

Bad habits are like a comfortable bed: easy to get into and hard to get out of.

QUILTING TIPS

Quilts are like scrapbooks we can wrap around ourselves.
Salvage quilt scraps from childhood clothing, blankets, aprons,
and so on to preserve your memories of bygone days.

- Cut quilt templates out of sandpaper. The sandpaper won't slip as you cut out your fabric.
- To sharpen your rotary cutter, slice through several layers of aluminum foil.
- Keep a cup close to your workspace to collect scraps of fabric and thread. Or tape a paper lunch bag to the edge of your sewing table to catch thread and other trash.
- Thread a whole pack of needles at once onto 1 spool of thread. Knot the end to prevent them from falling off. Each time you need new thread, pull the required length through a needle; then cut the thread from the spool and knot the end.
- Old blankets can be used for the middle (batting) of a quilt.
- A flat sheet makes a nice and durable backing for a quilt.
- When basting quilt layers together using long stitches, be sure to use a thread that contrasts with the quilt so you can easily see it and remove it later.
- When marking for echo quilting, use dots instead of a line. Dots don't pull the fabric or cause distortion.
- When hand quilting on a hoop, baste a piece of fabric onto the edge of the quilt to extend the grip on the hoop and to keep the edge straight and taut.

- To protect fingers from pricks, wrap them with masking or adhesive tape.
- To keep your thimble on your finger, cut a fingertip from a latex household glove. Slip the glove tip over your finger before putting on the thimble.
- Roll a piece of duct tape around your fingers, sticky side out, to use as a magnet for pieces of thread—even pet hair.
- To hold strips of binding out of the way while hand stitching, use paper binder clips or butterfly hair clips.
- If fabric has been scorched by ironing, dip it in weak tea to conceal the spot.
- Don't wash a quilt too often and never dry-clean it. Most often all that is necessary to freshen a quilt is some time outside on a shaded clothesline.
- To store an old quilt, use a prewashed white cotton pillowcase as a bag.
- When storing quilts, refold them periodically. Having the folds fall in different places prevents them from causing permanent marks on the quilt.
- To air a quilt, place it on a mattress pad or several sheets and cover it with another sheet to prevent fading and protect it from debris. Place it outdoors in the shade.
- To comfort sore fingers, soak them in a mixture of magnesium salts and warm water or in alum water.

If we don't cut the peace pattern right, we will have scraps.

Knitting Tips

The simple act of knitting, of counting stitches and rows, losing oneself in the rhythm of pattern repeats, and the joy of watching a lovely piece of handiwork emerge, helps release tension and allows one to forget, if only for a moment, the realities of life.

- If you don't have access to a computer and printer to enlarge your knitting patterns, purchase one of those page-sized magnifier sheets and position it over the pattern.
- The dye lot number on a yarn label indicates that all yarns bearing that lot number were dyed in the same vat at the same time. Always purchase enough yarn in the same dye lot number to ensure a uniform color in your finished work.
- Some needles don't have the sizes marked or printed on them. Determine the size with a needle gauge tool and, using a fine-tipped permanent marker, write the size on the knob at the end of the needle or directly on the needle body. The larger the needle, the larger the completed stitch will be.
- Don't have a point protector? Doubled or tripled bulky rubber bands rolled onto the ends of the needles will help keep your work from slipping off.
- Slip your skein of working yarn inside a knee-high nylon stocking to keep it clean and free from tangling.

- Large, clean plastic coffee containers make excellent yarn ball holders. Pop your ball of yarn inside, set it beside your chair, and knit away. No more chasing that wily ball of yarn across the floor. (This is also a wonderful excuse to drink lots of coffee.)
- If your stitches keep slipping off metal needles, try switching to wooden, bamboo, or plastic needles, which provide a little more grip.
- Keep a small crochet hook handy for picking up dropped stitches.
- Bobby pins make dandy stitch markers. You can also use bobby pins to hold seams together before stitching.
- If your bound-off edges always end up too tight, next time try using a larger needle to bind off. This will make the edge a bit looser and provide more give.
- Toss some fingernail clippers into your knitting kit. They make great yarn cutters and take up less room than a pair of scissors.
- When giving a knitted gift, snip the care information from the yarn label and attach it to a pretty card. Slip the card into an envelope and include it with the item. This way the recipient will know how to properly care for their new handcrafted treasure.

Blessed is the close-knit family whose bonds of love extend to each one in the home and to each and every friend.

MISCELLANEOUS TIPS

Therefore whosoever heareth these sayings of mine, and doeth them, I will liken him unto a wise man, which built his house upon a rock.

MATTHEW 7:24

Open Windows

Use fans and open windows more days in the year than you use the air conditioner—and welcome the outside sounds and smells indoors. Even a house needs to breathe sometimes.

Prayers

Prayers in the morning start each day on the right path.
Prayers at night help the mind and body relax.

Verbalize

Know what's important to you and voice your priorities. Don't expect others to read your mind. We waste a lot of energy and emotion on unspoken feelings that never get resolved. So talk it out.

Sabbath Rest

Take a Sabbath day (or at least a block of several hours) once a week. This day lets the body and mind fully rest and is a good time for recharging the spirit too.

Less Is More—Possessions

It has been said that we can become a slave to our possessions. The more we own, the more we have to take care of in storing, cleaning, fixing, replacing, and more. Consider how having less stuff will actually free your time, money, and worries.

One business policy that never needs changing is honesty.

STATIC

For static in your dress, rub hand lotion on your legs.

MIRIAM BYLER, SPARTANSBURG, PA
NATHAN AND ANNA FISHER, SALISBURY, PA

SOCK SORTING

Mark your children's socks with a paint marker. Make 1 dot for the oldest child's socks. Add a dot for the next oldest child's socks. If you hand them down, add more dots to match the younger child's mark.

RACHEL MILLER, MILLERSBURG, OH

FRAYED SHOESTRINGS

When shoestrings lose their plastic tips, dip them in clear fingernail polish.

DRAWERS

To organize your drawers, use empty wipe or tissue boxes. Take off the lid or top. Place enough boxes in each person's drawer for containing socks, underwear, and/ or handkerchiefs. No need to fold all the wash. Who wears their clothes folded? Having a small drawer to pitch in washcloths instead of folding them works too.

RACHEL MILLER, MILLERSBURG, OH

SLIPCOVERS

Old pillowcases can be repurposed. Cut a small slit in the short, closed end. Slip the pillowcase over a clothes hanger to protect special clothes.

SAGGY CALENDAR

If your wall calendar wants to sag in at the top edges, use paper clips to hold the pages together and upright. Or use a plastic clothes hanger that has a clip on both sides to hold up each top corner.

JUDITH ANNE MILLER, FREDERICKTOWN, OH

SLOW BURN CANDLES

Keep candlesticks or birthday candles in the freezer for a day before using and they will burn more slowly and evenly.

HOMEMADE POTPOURRI

1½ cups dried orange rind	1 tablespoon whole allspice
1½ cups dried apple peel	3 tablespoons whole cloves
1½ cups dried lemon rind	2 small star anises (optional)

Mix all ingredients and store in jar. Use a spoonful or two in a saucepan of water on low heat. Makes the house smell good.

RUBY MILLER, AUBURN, KY

MANNERS MATTER

Teach your children proper manners and practice them daily in the home as well as in public.

FORGIVE

Always be willing to forgive—and to accept forgiveness. True peace comes only when we can face our mistakes and be reconciled with others in our lives.

WELCOME CHANGE

Change opens us to new possibilities, new experiences, new lessons in life. So celebrate the changes that come your way and go with the flow.

*Don't be so busy making a living
that you forget how to live!*

DAVID AND LAURA BYLER, NEW CASTLE, PA

Glue Issues

When glue thickens in the bottle, add a few drops of vinegar. Glue spots may also be dissolved with vinegar.

Recycled Containers

Extend the life of food containers from things like yogurt, sour cream, and margarine by using them for storing leftovers and freezing food.

Tin Cans

- Recycle your tin cans to make cute buckets. Gallon, half-gallon, and quart cans make great buckets for children to carry water. Punch 2 holes in the top and fasten a strong wire to make a handle.
- Use a tin can with a sharp edge as a quick chop. Or use cans to collect bugs off plants.
- Short cans can be used to make pincushions. Crochet a bowl the same size as your tin. Slip it over the tin, leaving the top open. Fill the bowl with a good amount of hair that you combed out. Cut a cloth the right size for the top and tightly stitch it onto the yarn. The tin is covered, and you have a place for your pins. The hair keeps the pins rust-free.

Mrs. Levi Miller, Junction City, OH

Simple Funnel and Bucket

Reuse milk jugs by cutting the tops off for funnels and using the lower parts with handles for buckets.

Storing Knives

To store knives, clean them and rub them with a little cooking oil. Fold them individually in flannel or a chamois cloth.

Storing Suitcases

When storing suitcases, keep a bag of dried lavender or other sachet inside to keep them from becoming musty.

Window Screens

To seal small holes in window screens, apply 2 to 3 coats of clear nail polish. Let it dry completely between each application. This also works great for small cracks in windows.

MIRIAM BRENNEMAN, MORLEY, MI
LIZZIE CHRISTNER, BERNE, IN

Hanging Curtains

When putting up curtains, slip something like a rubber finger guard over the end of the curtain rod so that the curtain material slides easily without snagging.

Salvaging Old Sheets

If the middle of a sheet is worn out, use the sides to make pillowcases, hankies, and more.

ROSIE SCHWARTZ, SALEM, IN

Rag Bag

An old T-shirt rag will last 100 times longer and preserve more trees and money than buying paper towels each week. Start a rag bag from old clothes and towels instead of throwing them away.

Drop Cloths

Keep old sheets and blankets for drop cloths when painting or to cover strawberries and other plants when in danger from frost. If the cloths get wet, dry them on the clothesline. No need to wash them often.

MIRIAM BYLER, SPARTANSBURG, PA

Painting Tips

- When you are painting and want a whiter white, add 2 teaspoons black paint per gallon of white.

MIRIAM BRENNEMAN, MORLEY, MI
LACY GLICK, MILL HALL, PA

- To keep bugs off fresh paint, mix a little peppermint oil, citronella oil, or vanilla into the paint.
- When painting, tape or glue a paper plate to the bottom of the paint can to catch any drips or spills.

Wallpaper Removal

To remove wallpaper, mix 1 heaping tablespoon saltpeter and 1 gallon hot water. Apply freely to wallpaper, keeping water hot. The paper will peel off easily.

Varnish Remover

1 cup ammonia
1 cup baking soda
1 cup Borax
2 cups water

Mix all ingredients together. Paint on a piece of furniture with paintbrush. Let this soak for 30 minutes. Wash off with soapy water. If it dries before you get it washed off or if the varnish doesn't all want to come off the first time, just brush another layer on and wash off again. This is a very simple and easy way to get that old varnish off a piece of furniture that you want to refinish.

Mrs. Monroe Miller, Blanchard, MI

The secret of success in conversation is to be able to disagree without being disagreeable.

Septic Aid

Save orange peels and put them in the septic tank and outhouse. It helps the waste decay and works as a deodorizer.

AARON AND EMMA GINGERICH, BREMAN, OH

Lanterns

Do not throw away your old lantern generators. Soak them in vinegar overnight. The next day, blow them out with an air hose. The generator might not be worn out but merely full of dirt.

MALINDA M. GINGERICH, SPARTANSBURG, PA

Debt Busters

Extra money from bonuses, tax returns, rebates, and gifts should go toward paying off debt before spending on entertainment and pleasure items.

Safety Net

Start a savings account and put aside what you would need to live on for at least three months if your income should be severed.

Hard Times

To survive hard times, I think the old motto holds true today: use it up, wear it out, make it do, or do without.

EMMA KURTZ, SMICKSBURG, PA

Use It Up First

Don't buy more of something before you use what you have on hand—for example: fabric, wrapping paper, and stationery.

Buy Old

Shop antique stores, yard sales, and flea markets when you need something. Old things were made better than today's disposable plastic and may still have a lot of life left in them.

End-of-Season Bargains

Plan ahead and buy things you need at the end of a season when items are discounted.

Fire Starters

Fill an egg carton loosely with wood shavings. Pour melted candle wax or paraffin over the shavings. Let harden and break into pieces and use to start a fire.

Mrs. Levi Miller, Junction City, OH

Sit by a Bonfire

There is something about fire that draws us and comforts us. Being out under the stars and surrounded by nature is relaxing. There is also something strangely liberating in the experience of cooking our food over open flames.

Plan for Emergencies

Have a set plan for emergencies. Create a portable emergency kit that you can grab and take with you. Pack a large kit of supplies for surviving a long period of time without electricity and other utilities.

Know Your Neighbors

Create a network among neighbors so you can call on someone close if you should have a problem.

Ask for Help

There is no need to be a lone ranger. It's okay to ask someone to help you complete a project, learn a new skill, or whatever it may be. Most people around us are not aware of our need until we ask for help.

The Secret to an Amazing Life

Go to bed early.

Don't eat too much.

Work hard.

Help people.

Don't let anything get your goat.

Tend your own business.

Be enthusiastic.

Always keep God in your mind.

Ruth Byler, Quaker City, OH

Dig your neighbor out of trouble, and you'll find a place to bury yours.

Index of Contributors

INDEX OF TIPS BY KEY SUBJECT

OTHER COOKBOOKS AVAILABLE FROM WANDA E. BRUNSTETTER'S AMISH FRIENDS

Wanda E. Brunstetter's Amish Friends Cookbook

Wanda E. Brunstetter's Amish Friends Cookbook: Volume 2

The Best of Amish Friends Cookbook Collection (repack from V1 & 2)

Wanda E. Brunstetter's Amish Friends Cookbook: **Desserts** (HB)

Wanda E. Brunstetter's Amish Friends **Christmas** *Cookbook*

Wanda E. Brunstetter's Amish Friends **Harvest** *Cookbook*

Amish Cooking Class Cookbook

Wanda E. Brunstetter's Amish Friends **Gatherings** *Cookbook*

Wanda E. Brunstetter's Amish Friends **Christmas** *Cookbook* (revised and expanded)

Wanda E. Brunstetter's Amish Friends **Farmhouse Favorites** *Cookbook*

Wanda E. Brunstetter's Amish Friends **from Scratch** *Cookbook*

Wanda E. Brunstetter's Amish Friends **Healthy Options** *Cookbook*

Wanda E. Brunstetter's Amish Friends **Baking** *Cookbook* (repacked, reprinted recipes)

Wanda E. Brunstetter's Amish Friends **4 Seasons** *Cookbook*

Wanda E. Brunstetter's Amish Friends **No Waste** *Cookbook*

Wanda E. Brunstetter's Amish Friends **One-Pan Wonders** *Cookbook*